M000100127

Kudos for

RECURRENCE

The plot of this novel is so interesting and thrilling that I want to be careful not to give details away! Although the violent and sexual content of Recurrence is quite shocking, it is absolutely necessary in order to fully understand the impact that this life is having on John's mind. Norem's prose flows beautifully and it often feels like John is speaking directly to us through the lively and impactful dialogue.

Reviewed by K.C. Finn for Readers' Favorite

5 STAR AWARD

Also by Dave Norem

Tough Old Man Uncle Mack

Daniel Tanning Confederate Spy

Sinkhole

Papertown

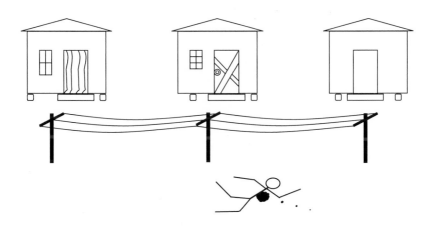

Dave Norem

ISBN 978-1-54397-667-0 eBook 978-1-54397-668-7

The tall, bearded killer lay face down in the weeds behind the chosen shack, knife gripped in his right hand. Discarded farm equipment parts and pieces surrounded him and his outline blended in with the odd shapes. He wanted the man from this shack but knew he wouldn't be able to catch him at an outhouse like the last one. A shape appeared at the side of the shack and he lowered his face to the ground as the figure slowly walked his way.

It was the kid. He wanted a kid all right, but not this one. He wanted the kid who lived in the house on the other side of the shacks, the smart ass. He wanted to make that one sweat before he took him though. Now, this kid was almost on top of him.

"Let not any one pacify his conscience by the delusion that he can do no harm if he takes no part, and forms no opinion. Bad men need nothing more to compass their ends, than that good men should look on and do nothing."

John Stuart Mill 1867

CHAPTER 1

George Rickson felt sorry for the poor kids who lived on the next property over, in Papertown. He knew that someday, something terrible would happen over there.

Everyone living in Papertown had it rough in their one-room, tarpaper-covered shacks, some with no windows and one or two with no doors. His home had three rooms and his family had their own outhouse.

Papertown residents who didn't have a door hung old, brown, wool army blankets over the doorway. During winter all of them heated their shacks with homemade stoves built from old car parts, oil barrels, boiler kettles or whatever else they could get their hands on.

The people in the shacks with doors tried to keep the rats out by covering the knotholes and rat holes with old can lids or license plates, nailed on with leftover roofing nails. Most of the people had little or no furniture and slept on old pee-stained mattresses on the slabwood floors. All of the kids in a house would have to share a mattress. Most of them never hung around long enough for age to make any difference, and seldom did any of those who left ever return.

Sometimes George would hear one or more of the kids in Papertown scream in the night from a rat running over them or biting them. Sometimes the screams were from something worse but George didn't know what happened to them. He was lucky enough to sleep on a rollaway bed with only his little brother, Linden, to kick him in the back.

Papertown was a conglomeration of eight shacks, none with electricity. Each was about twelve feet wide by fourteen feet deep. They were built in a row close enough together to spit from one to another and shared a common outhouse at the far end. No one was sure which end had the advantage.

Some of the shacks rested on poles lying on the ground while others stood on concrete blocks under the corners. Dogs or cats lived underneath the shacks, depending on how high they were off the ground. Chickens lived and died on the bare ground surrounding the shacks. There was no chicken house. There had been one before the shacks were built, but the roof had caved in and the lumber, along with the remains from a small barn, were scavenged in support of newer construction.

At night, some of the chickens, able to fly, roosted on the clothesline posts. Others roosted on whatever else they could find to keep them off the ground. If they roosted on nearby cars, of which there were few, plastering their goo on fenders, hoods or windshields, they were the first to die.

The shacks squatted behind the Corbetts' house, next door to the Rickson home, and no more than fifty yards away. The row was perpendicular to the road, with the doorways facing the Rickson property. The paved county highway passed in front of the two houses, with the Rickson house slightly farther back. Corbetts' driveway curved around the house on the far side, and the Corbetts parked behind it. The Rickson driveway was between the houses, straight in from the road, and ended just short of their open back porch.

The houses and shacks fronted a dense forest farther back from the road, while sparse redbrush, scrub pines and tall weeds filled the seventy-yard distance between. Fallow fields of the same lay on either side of the houses for a quarter-mile or more in either direction.

When facing the woods, it seemed impenetrable with great tangles of briars and brambles. On closer inspection there were occasional entry paths, made first by animals and then later by humans in pursuit of them. In the early 1950s, they were seldom used by man.

The Rickson home was sided with thick, light-gray asphalt siding with a slight pink cast to it. The two-story Corbett house was covered with tan, faux-brick, roll siding. The Ricksons' outhouse was painted battleship gray with black trim around the door, corners and windows. It had a peaked roof with black shingles, and a small, square, turned-at-an-angle glass window up near the eaves on each side for light. Pete Rickson had cut a quarter-moon profile a foot high into the door near the top. Ventilation was through a gap at the bottom of the door, the cut moon, and the open eaves under the roof overhang.

The Papertown outhouse was covered with bare, gray, weathered, overlapping slabwood nailed vertically. Cracks between the boards, and a six-inch square opening above the door were sufficient for ventilation. The flat roof, covered with tarpaper, sloped downhill from the front. The roof carried an uneven overhang of about nine inches all around, but it wasn't cut square, making it look like a lid not quite in place. George had heard people complaining about the seat covered with rain or snow coming in through the square opening.

The larger Corbett home had indoor plumbing supported by a septic tank opposite the driveway. A truck had previously caved in the top of the septic tank, so now the area around it was fenced in. The Corbetts took advantage of the fencing and maintained a small, thriving garden within its confines.

Mr. Corbett, a tall, solid-looking man with gray, wavy hair and creases in his forty-year-old, clean-shaven face owned all of Papertown. He took care of the local cemetery and built concrete forms for anyone who wanted to pay for them. His older brother, who never appeared at the Corbetts' or Papertown, owned a fair-sized sawmill. One of its byproducts was the slabwood lumber Mr. Corbett liked for his building projects. Most of the men living in Papertown worked for Mr. Corbett or his brother doing odd jobs, digging graves, cutting weeds, or in the sawmill.

George's dad, Pete Rickson, said that they all had an agreement with Corbett, and Corbett had all of them.

Papertown kids had ragged clothes and some didn't have shoes. George's clothes were sometimes patched but were not ragged. He didn't eat anything outside because he didn't want to make the other kids hungry. The few times he'd tried eating a peanut butter sandwich or an apple outside, the little McDews kids hung around him big-eyed and drooling with their stomachs growling. The kids, two boys and a girl were some of the poorest of the lot. The McDews' shack was closest to the Ricksons' and these kids were George's favorites.

Their dad, Fowler McDews, was a drunken lout who was always cussing out his wife and kids and sometimes beat them inside the shack. George could hear it from his back porch or from inside the house if a window was open. Fowler was tall and thin with dark hair, a long nose, and a bony face. Some people said he was chicken-breasted, but George didn't know about that.

George's dad said that if he ever caught McDews beating his wife or kids outside he would knock the shit out of him. He didn't want to go to jail for going into his house though. He had asked Mr. Corbett why he let them stay and Mr. Corbett said that Fowler McDews was the best gravedigger he ever had.

Then, one day something bad did happen. A woman walking to the store found a little girl's body in a ditch half-a-mile away. George first heard about it at school. He was standing in front of his locker with the door open and overheard older kids talking about it from the other side of the door. One of the kids said, "Man, she had been *ravaged!*"

"Whatever that means," someone else said. Two or three of them laughed, and then they all left.

It turned out that the eight-year-old girl was not from Papertown but from a house more than a mile away. That night when his parents thought he was sleeping; George heard his parents talking about it. His mother said, "It wouldn't surprise me if Fowler McDews had something to do with it."

His dad responded, "There's a good chance of it, but if he's such a good gravedigger, why didn't he bury her while he was digging graves?"

"She's not the only little girl that's gone missing. Maybe he was too drunk," his mother replied. After that, they lowered their voices and George never heard any more.

George was a handsome boy with dark, curly hair, deep-blue eyes and a cleft chin. His dad, Pete Rickson, was a big burly man with wiry dark-brown hair, a stiff full moustache, piercing dark eyes, and a no-nonsense manner. He preferred not to talk much, letting others commit themselves before agreeing with them or setting them straight.

Pete Rickson was the local area union representative for the railroad and was responsible for inducting new employees and the settling of any disputes. For a long time now, nothing had been moving and there was only one man working there other than himself. Rickson's job included both passenger and freight depots at the county seat, so the two of them were shuttled back and forth. He was also in charge of full or part-time hiring for yard or siding work and freight handling. This was an important position for the area even when there wasn't any real work.

George's mother, Lois, was a taller-than-average woman but not overly tall. She had shoulder-length, light-brown hair, dark, amber-colored eyes and a winning smile. A light-brown mole on her left cheek gave her a vulnerable look. She was well endowed without looking chubby or sexual. Her manner was always pleasant but subdued and people of all ages liked her immediately. Little brother, Linden, three years younger than

George, was small for his age and had lighter hair. He also had his mother's amber-colored eyes and delicate features.

Sometimes in the evening, George would see Mr. McDews follow one of the other Papertown women to the outhouse. Once there was a big fight with another man who lived there; and Fowler McDews gave the man a bad beating. That was one of the rare times in the evening when he wasn't drunk. The other people were gone the next day. Fowler McDews continued his drinking, usually sitting in the open doorway with his feet on the ground, a *Lucky Strike* hanging from his lips and a cloud of blue-gray smoke surrounding him.

One winter day, Ralphie McDews, the oldest of the kids, told George that their cousin had gotten into trouble and was coming to live with them for a while. Ralphie was blonde, blue-eyed and skinny with an undernourished look like his siblings.

The cousin, who showed up on a Saturday morning, was a girl about fourteen years old with a pouty-looking face, greasy brown hair and clothes two sizes too small. Her name was Earline and she looked at George like she wanted to see if his clothes would fit her. It gave him the creeps. Her skin was oily looking and pimply. George also noticed that she had big knockers.

That evening, as he was returning from the outhouse, George heard a big fight going on in the McDews shack. A few minutes later, he sneaked out onto his back porch to listen. Just as he got there, the McDews' door flew open and the two smaller children came running out into the snow, crying.

He heard Fowler say "Don't talk back to me you little bastard."

Afterwards George heard a couple of smacking sounds. Ralphie McDews flew through the doorway at about waist height, and landed on his back in the yard. The door slammed shut and George went over to where the other kids were looking at Ralphie. He was lying there moaning with blood all over his face. The door flew open again and George saw Fowler slap Mrs. McDews.

He said, "She's asleepin in our bed." Then he shoved her through the door backwards and slammed it shut again.

Mrs. McDews stumbled and fell on her rump, then quickly got to her feet and went over to where Ralphie was just getting up.

Annie McDews was a slender, ample-breasted, dishwater-blonde. She was pretty when she smiled, but that was seldom. Somehow, she always managed to keep herself clean looking.

George knew then that Fowler McDews was a truly evil man. George imagined driving a nail through his peter and into the chopping block. He knew that it would never happen though. McDews was a grown man.

"I'll go get my dad," George said.

Mrs. McDews shook her head, "No George, we'll be all right. Your father is a good man and he don't need this kind of trouble. Go back to your house and forget all about this. We'll pretend you weren't even out here."

She took her kids and went to Mr. Corbett's house. The next day three dressed-up strangers, two men and a woman came to the McDews shack. George didn't know who they were, but guessed that they were from the County. After a half-hour visit, they took Earline away in a green car. George never saw her again.

For the rest of the winter George stayed inside whenever any of the McDews family was outside. He felt bad for the kids but didn't know what he could do for them. Everybody said McDews drank, while his family starved.

CHAPTER 2

Somehow, by spring, Fowler McDews had gotten himself an old car. George didn't know what kind it was but it was hump-backed, with three chrome strips rising up over the trunk lid, and had two little windows up high in the rear. One Saturday George had walked the mile to Hastings' Store & Station to get some milk and eggs for his mother. Mrs. McDews came into the store as he was leaving and said "Hello George" as she walked by.

When he got outside, he noticed Fowler McDews at the gas pumps getting gas for the old car. George saw that the rear seat was out of the car, propped against a back fender, and the attendant was putting gas in a tank under the seat. McDews was in the front seat and had made the three kids get out of the back so the man could fill the tank.

The kids stood in a row at the back of the car with their eyes downcast. George was amazed to see that both boys, as well as the girl, were wearing flowered dresses with puffy sleeves. They were made of some crinkly, partially transparent material that had been popular for a couple of years. They were just transparent enough in the sunlight to see that Ralphie wasn't wearing any underwear. The other two kids were. All of them were wearing clodhopper work shoes that were too big for them and no socks.

Ralphie noticed George staring at him and turned beet red as he scuffed his toes into the dirt beside the car. George felt so mortified that seven and nine-year-old boys would be forced to wear dresses in public that he wanted to run over and start punching and kicking Fowler McDews right then and there. He knew this would probably get him killed but he felt cowardly for not trying. He left as humiliated as the McDews kids must surely have felt. Something had to be done about Fowler McDews.

George was mad now. He thought about Fowler beating his family, about the cousin and about the boys wearing dresses. He also recalled his parents saying McDews probably had something to do with the missing girls.

For days, George couldn't get the sights or the memories out of his mind and was too embarrassed to tell anyone about it. A week later, something happened to change things forever.

George was awakened to a roaring and then muffled thudding noises from the road out in front of the houses. He went into the kitchen in the dim light and looked at the clock. It was 2:30 AM. He pulled on his shoes and pants and went out onto the back porch to peer around the corner. He saw the McDews car sitting in the road in front of Papertown and a man George didn't recognize in the darkness pulling the back seat out of the car. The man dropped the seat on the ground and staggered up to the driver's window.

George heard him say "Wake up, Fowler, you drunk skunk." He staggered to the side, dropped to his knees, and threw up. After this, the drunk went off into Papertown and disappeared.

George waited a while then cautiously approached the car. He could hear Fowler snoring and smell the vomit from several feet away. When he got to the car, he could see that someone had thrown up on the back seat cushion that was lying on the ground. He also saw that McDews had an opened pack of *Luckies* and a *Zippo* lighter lying on the front seat on the passenger side.

George worked his way around the car and reached in for the lighter. Fowler was dead drunk and never heard a thing. George took the Zippo and went back down the path to his outhouse. A short time later George again approached the car after checking to be sure that everyone in his family was still asleep.

Fowler McDews was still snoring in his drunken stupor and hadn't moved. George eased into the back of the car and slowly and carefully removed the cap from the gas tank and laid it on the floor. Taking a length of toilet paper from his pocket, he poked the end down into the tank and stretched the paper to the outside of the car.

The hardest part came next. His hands were shaking so bad it took both of them to operate the Zippo. After making sure the paper was burning, he dropped the lighter on the ground and ran back to the outhouse, afraid he wouldn't have time to get into bed before everyone woke up.

For a while, he thought the fire had gone out and nothing was going to happen. He wondered what Fowler would do if he woke up and found the burned toilet paper leading to his gas tank. George started to go back to his house so he would be safe for morning but just as he was leaving the outhouse, he saw a flash of light and heard a loud whoosh, followed by a scream. He ducked back inside and pulled the door almost shut. Then he saw a huge ball of fire and heard a loud, thunderous boom. The inside of the outhouse lit up from light entering through the moon cutout and one window. Seconds later, he heard stuff hitting the ground. Then the outhouse dimmed as the fire diminished.

Emotion overcame him and he stayed in the outhouse until after the loud noises and voices faded. Several minutes more passed and he heard his mother's voice coming nearer, calling his name. He was never so glad to see her in his whole life. He told her he was in there when he heard the explosion.

No one ever suspected what happened. A few nights later he heard his father tell his mother that Fowler McDews was buried in a grave he had dug himself.

"A fitting end to him too," he said.

It seemed that Mr. Corbett always had a grave or two dug in advance in case one of the diggers got drunk the night before a burial and didn't show up...

CHAPTER 3

George Rickson was eleven years old when Fowler McDews died. His birthday was April 1st, but he never mentioned it to other kids, as he didn't want to hear the snide remarks or get into fights over it. When he was ten, he said to his mom that he was a fool's baby. His dad heard and smacked him a good one, knocking him halfway across the room with a hard slap. He never said it again.

Now, during the next two-and-a-half-year period, Papertown grew from eight tarpaper shacks to twenty. Two of the new shacks extended the existing row and the others were built facing the originals, their backs to the Rickson property. The outhouse at the end had been filled with deposits nearly to ground level and workers moved the outhouse twenty feet farther back. They covered over the old hole and mounded the dirt up over it, but people said the ground was squishy there, and most of the time they walked around it. Corbett's crew built a second outhouse behind the middle of the first row of shacks, on the side opposite the Rickson property. Pete Rickson had long before posted a *Rickson Family Only* notice on his own outhouse.

The growth of Papertown was due largely to the growth of the nearby sawmill, and the addition of Olsons' Tavern, near Hastings' Store & Station, less than a mile away. This kind of growth also brought a rougher crowd of both kids and adults.

By his initiation into his teens, George had grown also, too nearly as big as some of the men in Papertown. During this time-span, he made a new friend at school named Ollie Hartwell. Ollie was the same age as George and also had dark hair and blue eyes. His skin was almost snow white though, and he had light-tan freckles on his face, hands and arms.

Ollie had a brother named Claude, who was seventeen. Claude had brown hair and wasn't as tall as George or Ollie. He looked older and tougher though, being heavier and more muscular, with a few dark whiskers and a front tooth missing. He'd quit school at fifteen to work in the onion fields and later in the Corbett Sawmill.

The Hartwell brothers, and a sixteen-year-old sister named Lorraine, lived at home with their parents in a full-sized house half-a-mile from George. Lorraine had dark hair and white skin like Ollie's, but didn't have the freckles. She didn't smile much and George thought she had a mean look to her.

Claude's two years in the workforce enabled him to buy an old 31 International pickup truck that he used for odd jobs to supplement his meager income. His accumulated property included a canvas-covered, wood-strip canoe and a small, wooden flat-bottomed boat made from the first plywood George had ever seen.

On weekends in the summer, Claude, Ollie, George and several other boys would load both boats on Claude's truck. He had a wooden frame built up from the stake pockets to hold the canoe above the cab. The home-made flat-bottomed boat had to be tilted to fit into the bed of the truck and at least two boys had to ride in the back of the truck to counterbalance it so that it wouldn't fall out. This was all part of the fun and George was included. They went to lakes and gravel pits within a twenty-mile radius, and had a great time swimming and fishing. Part of the fun was diving from the boats and trying to capsize them and dunk whoever might be still in them.

One day a blonde-headed boy named Dean, who owned a car, went with them as part of their group; and they were able to take a float trip down the river. They spot-parked the car just upstream from where George lived and all loaded into the truck. They launched the boats several miles upstream. Afterwards, two of them used the car to retrieve the truck.

It was a warm, sunny, lazy day with all floras in their full splendor and the temperature in the mid-eighties. A couple of the mothers had packed food and bottled Kool-Aid into big lard cans. The boys were having a great time until they rounded a bend in the river and saw several people on the bank picnicking near a bridge. Where the group was gathered, thick, dark-green grass and daffodils covered the lightly-sloping gravel bank to the river's edge. The picnickers had 3-legged folding stools with canvas seats to sit on, and a folding aluminum table set up for their food.

The boys were wearing only their undershorts and the water was too shallow to climb into the boats. They crouched down behind them, hoping to drift and dog paddle past without being noticed.

It was already too late. One of the men on shore was hollering for them to get out of the water. They couldn't understand why he was so upset. His hollering had drawn the attention of the others including women and girls.

"Shit, what's he so cranked about," Claude said.

Before anyone could answer, Ollie let out a yell and they all found out. The man had fishing lines out and Ollie had his drawers hooked by one of them. The man almost lost his rod-and-reel and there was a battle for control between him and Ollie. The man was stronger but all of the boys were hanging onto the boat and for a minute, they thought the man might come into the river after them. Ollie was prone behind the flat bottom boat, hanging on with one arm over the side, buried under a seat to the elbow, alternately digging his heels into the gravel bottom for traction. With the other hand he was busy sacrificing his drawers. They all had a good laugh about it after they were around the next couple of bends and out of sight.

"At least the old fart won't go home empty handed. He got a pair of holey drawers. He never would have caught anything else in that shallow water," Claude said.

Ollie had been wearing a cap all day, even swimming. Now, when he got out of the water, he yanked if off his head and used it to cover his crotch. Everyone burst out laughing again.

"Hey Ollie, where'd you get the ridgeline haircut," Dean hollered.

"Muskrat Mullins," Claude hollered back. "He only charges a dollar, so that's where my old man makes him go." They all hollered and whooped. Everyone knew about Muskrat, one of only two barbers in town. He had a narrow, bushy, brown mustache above a receding chin and oversized, upper front teeth that seemed to overhang his lower lip. Gaunt, sunken cheeks with a perpetual three-day brownish-gray stubble accented the look. His own dark-brown, three-quarter-inch-long hair grew forward over his forehead in a rounded widow's peak.

Muskrat's specialty was flattop haircuts. He had a big, six-by-nine-inch comb that he would lay on top of a customer's head while he mowed off anything sticking up through it. The flattops were never level.

George told them about a time when his dad was in the chair getting a shave. "A boy about twelve-years-old stepped halfway into the open door and hollered, 'Hey Mr. He'll cut your throat!'

"Muskrat Muller chased the kid for a block-and-a-half with his long apron flapping around his knees, and a straight razor held aloft in his hand, before he ran out of steam. When he returned to his barbershop, Pete Rickson was long gone, the cape wadded up on the floor. "Dad finished his shave at home," George hooted.

Ollie's haircut was more of a butch, with ridges on the sides and back, as if the clippers had been stopping and restarting. "Hey, you want to hear a good one?" Claude hollered. Before waiting for a reply, he went on. "I was sitting in the barber chair and a guy stuck his head in the door and said, 'Bob Peters in here?' Nope, said Muskrat; just shaves and haircuts!"

They all roared, and then Ollie came up with one. "A little girl was in the barbershop eating a sucker, watching while her daddy got his hair cut. The barber glanced over at her and said, 'little girl, you've got hair on your lollipop.' She pulled the sucker from her mouth without looking at it. 'Yep, she answered, got titties too.'" All the boys roared at that one and catcalled back and forth about who it might be.

George learned to row, paddle and swim during these excursions. He also learned some new swear words and more of the boy talk about girls and sex. At first, he was shocked at what he was hearing. When they discovered he was a novice at this, he caught a lot of good-natured kidding.

The kidding finally died out one weekend. Attention was diverted when Ollie told about Lorraine's brassiere. The day before, their dad saw it in the laundry with big greasy handprints on both cups. Lorraine had a twenty-year old boyfriend who worked at a filling station and spent most of his time there under the grease rack.

Their dad was so mad when he saw the handprints that he loaded his shotgun to go after the boyfriend. Lorraine was laying on the floor crying and hanging onto her daddy's leg while he was trying to get out the door. Their mother finally intervened and the boys were sent away, leaving just Lorraine and her parents to work things out.

All of the boys at the swimming hole got a big kick out of this story except for the brothers. The rest of them all wanted to see the evidence. Lorraine's best features had already been noticed.

Claude said, "Well don't even think about going near her now. If she's pregnant, the old man will kill that grease monkey and she'll be an old woman before she gets out of the house."

A week later, George was in the Hartwells' back yard waiting for Ollie to finish his chores. He found a pair of homemade stilts leaning up against a shed and decided to try them out. He went staggering across the yard on them and wound up against the back wall of the house right next to a small, open window. He glanced inside and saw Lorraine, naked from the waist up, bent over a laundry sink washing her hair in front of the window.

His bump against the wall alerted her and she rose up with her long hair wadded up in both hands at the back of her head. She gawked back at his big-eyed face, open-mouthed, with her elbows straight out to the sides. Before he could leap down from the stilts, she burst out laughing. George couldn't get away fast enough. The image of her huge breasts, nipples like fingertips pointing right at him, and the tangle of dark hair in her armpits burned into his mind. When Ollie came out, George was waiting down the street, several yards past their driveway. Ollie never said anything but he had an evil grin the rest of the day.

Just after the end of his summer of fun with the Hartwells, this part of his life came to an abrupt halt. On a Saturday that he was ordered to stay home and start laying up wood for the winter, the other boys went to the lake without him.

With both brothers in the cab of the truck and three boys in back, they rounded a bend and met an oncoming fuel-oil truck that was over the centerline by a wide margin. Claude ran off the road to avoid a head-on collision and the right front wheel hit a boulder hidden by the weeds. The truck tipped over on its side and then rolled down an embankment. Two of the boys riding in the truck bed were thrown through the air, slammed against tree trunks, and killed instantly. The other boy in back was thrown clear and suffered only a few scrapes and bruises.

Claude had a broken arm and some cuts from broken glass. The steering knob knocked his right thumb out of joint when he hit the boulder. Ollie was thrown partway out of the open passenger side window when the truck tipped over and the roofline of the cab broke his back when it rolled.

George saw him only one other time, nearly a year later. He found out then that Ollie had been in the hospital for several months and was paralyzed from the chest down.

Claude was banned from the family home and had left for parts unknown.

In the meantime, George himself had been banned from association with the Hartwells "and any other *Motorized Hellions*," by his dad.

George understood that he probably would have been killed too if he'd been with them. With Ollie and the truck both out of the picture, the banishment wouldn't have been necessary.

CHAPTER 4

George was still older than most of the kids in Papertown, but some were as big as he was. One of them was a tow-headed bully named Robert Williams. Robert had a lumpy-looking head that bulged out over his eyes and ears as if the top had been smashed down with a huge wooden mallet. At thirteen, he was a year younger than George, but looked five years older. He liked to hit smaller kids with a raised knuckle at the bony part of their arm, between biceps and shoulder. It didn't bother him to hit girls too when no one else was looking. He would also take money and smash toys the other kids might have. Money was little and toys were few in Papertown.

Robert didn't try to pick on George though. There was something about George that kept the bullies at a slight distance. George himself didn't bother them, as long as they didn't bother him.

George did have some feelings for the McDews kids and kept an eye out for them, giving them gentle warnings about staying away from the rougher kids. The car fire three years before had made a big change in their lives. These kids had grown also, but Ralphie, the oldest at twelve, was still small for his age.

Kids were not the only bullies. There were both men and women who would take advantage of the smaller or weaker. Deeter Jompson and his wife, Molly, were good examples. Deeter was average in height but had broad shoulders and rock-hard looking muscles on his arms, shoulders and back. He had big hands and knuckles for his size and a predatory look with his craggy features, square jaw and dark, bushy hair. He would bum cigarettes, money and beer from the other men and would threaten or hit them if they refused or asked to be paid back. George had heard his parents talking about Deeter being an ex-con who had killed a man with a piece of pipe and done time for manslaughter.

Molly, a tall, overly endowed redhead with blotchy skin, had been seen more than once stealing other women's underwear off the clotheslines strung between the rows of shacks. She'd been confronted once and had slapped the skinny accuser, knocking her flat. The woman scrambled away without another word. That evening, the woman's husband went to the Jompson shack and Deeter met him at the doorway with a beer in his hand.

After hearing what it was about, he stepped out saying, "Don't call my wife a thief, asshole."

The man stepped back and Deeter followed. He hit the man on the head and then in the face with the beer bottle, which didn't break. This was still enough advantage for Deeter to continue hitting and kicking the man until long after he was down. Oddly, more than half of the bystanders were cheering him on. A fight was free entertainment regardless of right or wrong.

Sometimes Deeter would come home from the tavern drunk and start cussing Molly, calling her a "two-bit whore" and other names. She would tear into him hitting and scratching and they would fight until both were on the ground in front of their shack in the dirt. Then they would go inside their doorless shack holding each other up, and drape a blanket over the doorway.

In a few minutes everyone around could hear them grunting like hogs. She would be moaning and saying, "Keep that bird in the nest, Deeter. Keep it in there, Honey." Or sometimes, "Give me your bird, baby." This might last for nearly an hour, depending on how much they'd had to drink. George thought it was hilarious that she called it a bird. He thought that Molly calling hers a nest was probably appropriate. Little did he know that he would eventually find out for himself.

One afternoon George heard a commotion near the newer outhouses in Papertown. He found a ring of kids surrounding Robert Williams and Ralphie McDews. The two were darting in and out at each other in a fistfight.

Both boys had their shirts off. Ralphie wasn't nearly as big as Robert and his ribs stuck out like ridges under his chalk-white skin. Both already had bloody noses. Robert would rush in and try to grab Ralphie who would dodge out of the way and hit or kick when he got close. Robert was trying to pummel Ralphie as he had others, and it wasn't working this time. George watched but didn't interfere.

Robert stepped back from one of his lunges and said, "Now you're going to get it McDews." He pulled a pocketknife out of his pants and pried open the blade in one move. All the kids around them fell silent but stayed in place. Robert had stabbed several smaller dogs and kittens since he'd lived there, killing a kitten and a chicken for no reason at all.

He made a lunge at Ralphie, who dropped to the ground and rolled away, coming back up into a crouch. On Robert's second lunge, George started to step in but Ralphie threw a handful of dirt he had grabbed during his roll. He lobbed it into Robert's face, causing him to back off. Robert glanced at George while he swiped at his face. "Stay out of this Rickson."

George stepped between them anyway just as another knife, with the blade open, came skittering across the ground from the crowd, toward

Ralphie's feet. "Go ahead Ralphie," Robert said with a dirty grin as he wiped his watery eyes.

Ralphie grabbed up the knife and George said, "Don't."

"I'll be OK," Ralphie said, and moved around George to face Robert.

Now, they again faced-off in readiness.

George stepped toward Robert just as they moved. Both Robert and Ralphie were lunging forward with knife in right hand and left arm raised in defense. Robert sneaked a quick glance to the right, toward George, as he moved in.

Ralphie's knife went up under Robert's left arm, and buried to the hilt in his armpit. Robert screamed so loud that everyone froze for a moment and then kids ran in every direction scattering dogs and chickens.

Robert dropped to the ground on his right side, still screaming, with his left arm raised straight up with the bone handle of the knife sticking out from under it. There was a growing circle of blood around it. His legs began pumping, spinning him in a circle in the dirt, as if he were running around inside a barrel on his right side. He just kept circling and screaming with his arm in the air. George was hollering at him to stop moving while Ralphie stood there with his mouth open, looking down at him.

All of the other kids were gone.

Adults were running toward them from several directions. George knew that only the truth would work now.

Edgar Semms, another adult bully, stepped in. He was one of the bigger men in Papertown and had long, stringy, graying hair with close-set eyes. As big as he was, he always seemed to avoid Deeter Jompson.

Semms crouched down by Robert and grabbed his legs with one hand stopping him from spinning. He reached for the knife with the other.

"Don't!" George hollered, even though he didn't know what would happen or why he even yelled.

Semms glared up at him with rotten teeth and said, "Beat it kid that's my *Case* knife." His bully son, Junior was the one who had kicked the knife in toward Ralphie. A thought flashed through George's mind that rotten teeth seemed to run in the family. Junior was one of the kids both older and bigger than George.

Before anyone else could do anything, Semms yanked the knife out of Robert. A huge spray of blood covered Semms, Robert, and George's pants from the knee down. Robert screamed a higher pitched and even louder scream, which stopped abruptly.

His legs hammered the ground as Semms let go, cursing him, "You little son of a bitch."

Robert's whole body quivered from top to bottom and then back up. Then he stopped moving... forever. George could smell when his bowels and bladder let go.

Before the day was over, Papertown was as quiet as a tomb except for the clucking of the chickens as they pecked at the last of the bloody ground. Sheriff's deputies and Sheriff Parks, himself, a man of well over six-foot-four and almost three hundred pounds, had questioned everyone including George. The Sheriff was said to be bald but George had never seen him without his western-style, Smokey-the-Bear, hat. Dark hair framed his ears and the back of his neck below the hat. All of the Sheriff's deputies wore Smokey-the-Bear hats too.

George was grilled again that night at home and told the truth; that he had only tried to stop the fight. His parents made no comment and the Sheriff gave him a strange look with his seemingly bottomless eyes, as if trying to recall something from a distant past. Ralphie McDews was taken away by the deputies, leaving his mother and siblings in tears. George never saw him again.

CHAPTER 5

Shortly after the death of her husband, Annie McDews was given the job of housekeeper for the Corbetts, who owned Papertown and had expanded to several outside business interests as well. Annie still had two hungry mouths to feed, other than her own. Any source of sustenance was welcome. Her dresses and her children's clothes were either threadbare hand-me-downs or homemade from already worn or damaged material from larger garments. Shoes were saved for special occasions or cold weather.

Mrs. Corbett, a solidly built woman with a stern countenance, kept her long, iron-gray hair gathered in a roll on top of her head and seldom deviated from that style. She was deeply religious and believed her acts of charity put her closer to the Lord.

Mr. Corbett's motive was of a different nature. He was more prone to taking advantage of the weaknesses of the Papertown women, using his money and stature. More than one woman had fallen victim before Annie. Everyone living in the tarpaper shacks was desperate for any improvement in their family's standard of living, by whatever means. Any attention was a relief from the squalor they all lived in.

Annie was a hard worker and soon took on more of the Corbett household duties, including laundry and some of the cooking. She also took over weeding and gathering from the garden over the septic tank. She kept some of the vegetables for herself but only took those she could boil because of where they came from. This left more time for Mrs. Corbett to attend prayer meetings at the local widower preacher's home, and to visit with the other women of means in the area. She had her own car, a two-year-old Pontiac.

Mr. Corbett built Annie a platform for two washtubs at the edge of the shacks, across the driveway from his own two-story house and much farther back than the septic tank. This allowed her to do laundry for some of Mrs. Corbett's friends and even for some of the lazier Papertown women.

The Corbetts had an upstairs apartment they let Annie and her children live in. It had an outdoor stairway running down the back of their big house. More than once George had seen Mr. Corbett's profile in the upstairs window when Mrs. Corbett was gone.

After Ralphie was taken away, George began helping Annie with the wash water on weekends. The smaller McDews kids would take turns with the community hand pump, filling the washtubs from buckets they carried back and forth. They carried a full bucket between then, sharing the weight. During the warmer seasons, Annie washed the clothes in cold water with a washboard and soap powders in one tub, and then rinsed them in the other. Then she would wring them out by hand and hang them on the clothesline to dry.

During the winter, washings weren't as often and usually a fire was built under the platform holding one of the tubs. Water sloshing over the sides of the tub helped keep the platform from burning, but sometimes made it difficult to keep the fire going. After one family's washing was done, Annie and George would carry the tubs of dirty water out behind the shacks and dump them. This had been Ralphie's job and George felt bad that he was gone.

He had offered to help with the water one day as a way to find out what had happened to Ralphie. Annie assured him that Ralphie was all right and was staying with a farm family who took care of kids who got into trouble. In return, the kids all worked on the farm. She said that Ralphie was far better off than the rest of them. George liked Annie and her kids and continued to hang around and help on the weekends and talk to Annie.

One hot day George was standing across from Annie while she was rubbing clothes on the washboard and talking. Suddenly he realized that Annie had soaked the front of her thin cotton dress. He could see the outline of both of her breasts and the darker area around the nipples. He quickly glanced away while Annie kept right on talking. He felt the heat rise up his neck and hoped she wouldn't notice the red before he could leave. She continued talking about the farm she had been raised on and the similarities and differences between it and the one where Ralphie was staying. George plunged his hands into the cold rinse water and grabbed an article of clothing and began to wring it out. He hadn't touched the clothes before.

Annie glanced over at him, then away without saying anything more for a while. Finally, without looking up she said, "George, you don't have to do this you know. This is usually considered woman's work and I wouldn't want to embarrass you."

"Oh no, I don't care what anybody thinks. I just need something to do with my hands while I'm hanging around. Besides you could probably work faster with my help, so I might as well."

"What about the other kids?" she said.

"None of them are my age, at least none I care about, and the bigger people don't care what I do," he replied.

"Come on let's empty the water, George," was her response. As they were dumping the second tub, she glanced over at him with a quick, funny little smile, and then away. George's heart skipped a beat and he hoped he wasn't red again. Annie didn't seem to notice if he was. He felt numb.

On the way back she said, "You know I can't pay you for helping, don't you?"

"Oh, I know that. I just like talking to you ma'am," he said with his ears burning.

"Don't call me ma'am, George, my name is Annie."

George didn't say anything in response, and she said nothing more. He left as soon as they got back to the wash area.

The following weekend he was back helping Annie with the laundry again. There wasn't much talk this time. Before long, George noticed Annie was again soaked and this time he could tell for sure she wasn't wearing a brassiere. This wasn't unusual for the Papertown women, but to be wet was different.

George kept sneaking peeks at Annie as he helped rinse the clothes in the cold water. He could see that her nipples were swollen and pushing out the thin cotton of her dress. Annie appeared preoccupied and didn't seem to notice. After they emptied the second washtub, she pushed the damp hair off her forehead with a wrist and gave George a brief smile. The gesture enhanced her wet breast. George tore his eyes away and noticed small beads of sweat on her upper lip, and a tendril of blonde hair curling across her forehead. The effect gave her the appearance of a teenager.

"George, I have a little job for you if you want it. Old Mrs. James on the next road back has broken her arm and can't do laundry. They want me to come over there this afternoon and do it for them. They're paying me well enough that I can give you a quarter to help."

"Sure," said George, "I'd do it without the quarter." He could feel his ears burning again. "How did she break her arm?"

Annie said, "She was carrying a basket of eggs and the wind blew the barnyard gate shut on her when she wasn't looking," and then she smiled and turned away.

George went home to let his mother know that he would be gone to work on the James farm for the afternoon.

George and Annie cut through the woods behind Papertown and climbed over a couple of fences getting to the back of the James place. George sneaked quick peeks at her legs as she climbed over. He helped her get her dress unhooked once and got a good look. She was wearing an old pair of men's shoes that had belonged to her dead husband. Somehow, they only made her slender, bare legs look more attractive. Annie didn't say anything until they were almost there.

"George, I've been noticing you looking at me like you want something."

He could feel his face turning red. "I'm sorry," he said.

"It's OK, George, I really don't mind and it makes me feel good that a handsome young man might find me attractive. It's just that you're not quite a grown man yet in the eyes of the people around us. We'll have to avoid situations like this morning, where people might notice and start spreading rumors.

"There's people around here who don't like either one of us, and are jealous. Besides that, I'm not yet thirty years old and the only other man I'm around is a mean old man who helps me out just enough to keep me and my kids from starving or freezing."

George didn't mention that he had just turned fourteen.

They spent two hours at the James farm and George earned another quarter from Old Man James for splitting some firewood and hauling wood and water into the house. Mr. James was tall and bony looking with sloping shoulders accented by the blue and white striped bib overalls he wore.

To George, Mr. and Mrs. James looked oddly alike with their collar length wispy gray hair and long slender noses. They didn't smell alike though. Mr. James smelled like a combination of animals, manure and feed, while Mrs. James smelled like wood-smoke and bacon grease, with a hint of home-baked bread.

The Jameses lived in a saltbox house covered in white slate siding. The house wasn't big for its style, but still seemed too large for two people. Inside, while he was filling the wood-boxes, George noticed that they had nailed the door leading to the upstairs shut and tacked trim strips around the joints. He glanced up at the overhead ceiling register and saw that Mr. James had tacked a piece of white, painted tin over it. Otherwise, the house was neat and clean with adequate furniture. On either side of the door, several wooden pegs mounted in three-foot-long varnished maple boards held coats and scarves. The boards were in contrast to the painted, glossy-green plaster-and-lath walls. The pegs were crooked, pointing at different angles. *Strange people*, George thought.

George left Annie alone with the laundry, helping only with carrying the water. By the time they had finished, Mrs. James was fixing supper with her one good arm and they took the hint that it was time to leave.

Mr. James paid them on the porch and then went back inside for his meal. They had no sooner left the yard when it started to rain. At first, it was big, slow lazy drops. When George and Annie got beside the barn at the back of the farm, they ducked under the eaves. Then the skies opened up, first rain and then hail. Through it all, the sun still shone. Annie ran around to the open back door of the barn saying "Come on George, we deserve a break anyway."

He followed her into the cooler shade and they stood there alternately looking around for a place to sit and checking for rainbows. They could hear hogs in the lot on the other side of the barn squealing, fussing and banging against the side of the building. Electricity crackled through the humidity and then lightning struck nearby with a ball of fire, throwing a barrel of dirt into the air. The air resounded with a loud BOOM! The ground and the whole building shook. The hogs were all squealing an unearthly sound then, like the hounds of hell were after them. George had never heard fully-grown hogs squeal and yowl before.

Annie grabbed him and squeezed him tight, both of them were soaking wet. George's knees wobbled. He grabbed her too, to keep from going over backwards, and he could feel her wet body plastered against his. Annie grinned at him as she stepped back, both of her hands gripping his arms at the elbows. His hands were on her hips and he was staring at her wet chest.

The sun faded and the skies turned molten and pounded the earth in alternating bursts of frenzy with rain and hail, as if it hated it.

Annie pushed away and headed for the ladder leading to the haymow that was half-full of loose hay. She looked down at him when she was at the top of the ladder, catching him looking up under her dress, at her legs. She went on, saying, "Well, come on."

Rather than say anything, he followed her up the ladder and got an eyeful of thigh.

Annie sat down cross-legged with her dress just to her knees and said "Come on George, sit down. Do you have a girlfriend?"

"No, he said as he sat down in a similar position facing her, with his hands in his lap.

"What about Gwen Waller?" she said. "I heard something about you and her."

George found it hard to speak, and hesitated before answering. "She hung upside down from the railing behind the school once and showed me what she had. Her underpants were stained and dirty looking and I don't really like her anyway."

Annie laughed and said, "I'm not wearing any underpants George, do you want to see what I have? Have you ever been with a woman?"

"Yes, I mean no. I ain't been with a woman but I wouldn't mind seeing." He could feel the blood rushing to his neck and his crotch too.

She grinned and lifted her dress showing that she really wasn't wearing anything under it. "What do you want to do now George?"

"Do *it*, I guess," he said with his voice cracking.

"Well what are you waiting for?" she said, reaching over and grabbing him by the hair and pulling him toward her. "Don't you want to find out what it's like?"

George did: he rose to his knees and one hand and leaned toward her. She stopped him with a, "Wait." Then she stood and pulled the dress up over her head, her crotch right in front of his face. She turned halfway around, bent from the waist, and spread the dress over the hay. Then she turned to face him wearing nothing but the clodhopper shoes.

"The first time won't take long at all," she said as he dropped his pants and undershorts. She watched while he did, and then lay back. When he crawled on top of her, he wasn't sure he could hold it at all. She grabbed him by the back of the neck with one hand and raised a breast to his mouth with the other. "Here's what you've been gawking at Baby, now it's yours!" He reached and grabbed the other one, bracing himself with one hand as she thrashed around under him while he was trying to find his way. He lost it before he got there.

"Don't worry Baby, I can't let you come inside me anyway, she murmured directly into his ear. Wipe it off with your shirttail and try again. You can make it." Then, for the first time, she kissed him. The kiss was soft, alive and wonderful to him. Everything seemed to be happening at once.

She was right that he could make it again, and they stayed long enough for him to finish a second time. He barely removed himself from her in time. George became so emotional that he could only gasp. He hissed into her ear, "I love you; I love you." She patted him gently on the back of the head.

When they finished, the rain had stopped, the sun was shining, wisps of steam rose from the ground, and the earth smelled new again. Below them, the hogs had settled down and were back to their normal grunting and oinking.

When they left the barn, he peered around the corner and spotted six or seven black-and-white spotted hogs weighing at least two hundred pounds apiece. As the two of them started back, they spotted two rainbows.

On the way, George and Annie passed where the lightning had struck. It had blown a tall, slender, shagbark hickory tree up out of the ground. The crater was three feet deep and some of the upraised roots were charred on the ends, with wisps of smoke still rising. Ironically, that gave each of them a story to tell.

Annie and George kept up their trips to the James farm for a few more weeks before Mrs. James was able to take over her own chores. One Saturday afternoon, when they came back through Papertown, Molly Jompson was standing in her doorway leering at them.

"What you been teaching that boy out in the woods, Annie? I bet I could teach him things you never even heard of." Looking at George she said, "Honey, if you want to learn some good stuff just come see Molly."

Annie just smiled and ignored her while George cast a quick glance at Molly's lush figure. He looked away without saying anything until they were out of earshot, and then said, "She always looks dirty."

Annie touched his arm and then quickly withdrew the touch. "We've got to keep a distance."

After two more trips, the work at the James farm ended. They had no excuse to be alone and stayed apart for the rest of the summer, except for him helping her empty the wash water.

CHAPTER 6

Summer was exceptionally hot that year. George awoke before daylight one morning to strange noises and got out of bed in the pre-dawn gloom to see what it was. His parents had propped open both doors the night before when they went to bed and George found the whole kitchen full of roosting chickens. They were roosting on the yellow and white, Formica-topped table, the backs and seats of all four chairs, on the cook-stove and on the shelf of the Hoosier cupboard.

The chickens usually roosted in low branches in the nearby scrub trees or on top of whatever cars were around, so the dogs couldn't get to them. A spring held their outhouse door closed so that they couldn't get in there to roost.

He turned the light on and started throwing and chasing chickens out the door. Some had gotten into the main room where he slept with his little brother, Linden. When he began to chase them out, he saw the strip of light appear at the bottom of his parent's bedroom door. He knew his dad had reached up and pulled the string that was running from the bare-bulb, pull-chain ceiling-fixture to the top rail of the brown metal headboard of the full-sized bed. The squawking, screeching and commotion woke up everybody in Papertown.

George was slipping and sliding, holding onto the walls and furniture. Chicken poop was on every flat surface and the chair backs. The air was full of flying chickens, down and feathers. Linden was sitting up in bed crying, his "wah…wah…wah" adding to the din.

George's dad was standing in his bedroom doorway grasping the doorframe as if to hold himself up. He was barefooted, wearing only his overalls, with the hair on one side of his head standing on end. It was the first time George could remember his dad looking silly. Between chickens, George noticed that his dad was actually laughing. Then he burst out laughing too.

After getting all the chickens out and closing the doors, George had to wash his feet and hands at the outside pump. His mother cleaned up the mess inside, mopped the floors, and brought his shoes out to him. The Ricksons were the brunt of chicken and chicken-shit jokes and comments for some time to come.

The heat also brought on an extraordinary amount of baptisms. Mrs. Corbett and her preacher friend went on a campaign to get all the Papertown residents baptized. They even tried recruiting the Ricksons, but George's dad ran the preacher off, calling him a "charlatan."

The preacher preferred being called Reverend. He was a tall, thirty-something, mild-appearing man with wavy, light-brown hair that had gray around the temples. He always wore a tie, even when wearing overalls. He had long arms and big knobby hands and a prominent Adam's apple. He reminded George of Ichabod Crane in Washington Irving's *The Legend of Sleepy Hollow*.

George didn't care one way or another about the preacher, but thought the baptizing would be fun to watch. He found out they were doing it down by the highway bridge. He was there in time to watch the whole thing from a close vantage point, but not so close that they would try to grab him.

He was surprised at how many people showed up but realized there wasn't a lot to do around there on a Sunday afternoon. They started with the men first. Two men would hold them from the sides while the victim held a white handkerchief over his nose. The two men would then tip him over on his back and down under the water three times, as the preacher read his sermon and hit the key words, "Father!" "Son!" and "Holy Ghost!"

There was a liberal pause between each of the words, and again when the sinner was brought completely upright between dunkings. The assistants never lessened their grip though. Some of the men struggled and cursed trying to get out of it once they hit the water. They were held longer and dunked deeper for their efforts. Stronger men had been selected for the job.

George surmised that with most of them, the much-needed physical cleansing was doing more good than the spiritual one. There was a lot of hooting and catcalling from the other men and the older boys. The preacher and his helpers ignored all of this.

George found the most interesting part to be the women and teenage girls. Both assistants held them closer and the preacher stood closer too. The crowd went silent when this started and after the first one, more attention was paid to the previous victims wading to shore than to the ones getting the treatment.

The ones coming out had their clothes plastered to their bodies, showing most of what they had. All were wearing thin dresses and it looked like several had no underwear at all. Some had blankets waiting to be draped over their shoulders. Some of the male bystanders offered their shirts to a few, but none were accepted.

George tore his eyes away from some of the heftier ones to watch the next dunkings. He noticed they tipped the girls so far back that their feet came to the surface. He noticed also that sometimes the men had a different grip when they brought them back up. They were in chest deep water on the men but it was too deep for the shorter women and girls. The helpers supported them by hands passed under their arms and behind the knees, forming a cradle before the process even started. They moved the baptizing closer to shore only when they got to the smaller kids.

George had been to the churches a couple of times and was amazed at how fired up people got. He'd nearly been trampled once by a heavy woman who'd *gotten the ghost*. She had rolled right over the back of the pew in front of him and went charging down his row toward the center aisle without even giving people a chance to pull their feet up and out of the way. Her eyes were rolling wildly and she made George think of a half-crazed steer or a hog that'd been eating jimson weed.

He'd seen others tear their own clothes and pull out handfuls of their own hair. Sometimes they would rattle off some kind of senseless babble that others said was *speaking in tongues*. George had also seen the *laying on of hands* and he knew for certain that some of these people were faking. After that, he quit going.

CHAPTER 7

Toward the end of summer, Linden became very ill. His parents had taken him to the local doctor several times. Neither the doctor nor anyone else seemed to know what was wrong with him. His mother tried what remedies she knew, but to no avail.

One morning George reached over in bed to wake him up for school. Linden had been thrashing around most of the night, throwing the thin blanket off on the floor and keeping George awake until well after midnight.

George grabbed Linden's thin bare arm and, finding it cold and lifeless, he screamed out to his parents. His dad burst through the door completely naked. George could only point to Linden and shake his head.

His mother appeared and was nearly as naked as his dad, wearing only a half-slip and brassiere. He had never seen them like this before. Without seeming to notice him, they both knelt at the side of the rollaway bed beside Linden. His dad was shaking him by the shoulders. His mother had one hand on his dad's arm and the other on Linden's chest.

She was begging him to stop shaking Linden, saying, "Don't hurt him anymore, don't hurt him anymore!" Tears were streaming down her face.

George jumped from the bed in his undershorts, grabbed his pants and shoes, and ran from the house, forgetting his shirt. He didn't stop until he was deep into the woods and noticed the pain in his bare feet from sticks and stones, and in his legs from the sandburs he'd picked up along the way. He sat down on a downed tree trunk, wiped off his feet, and put his pants and shoes on.

He spent most of the day there, wandering around and looking at the birds and squirrels, at times he sat dozing propped up under trees. No one came looking for him. Late that day when he returned to the house, Linden was gone and his dad stayed in the bedroom with the door closed. His mother had been sitting at the table with a dazed look on her face. She got up and quietly fixed him something to eat without really talking to him.

While he was eating, she silently swabbed rubbing alcohol onto his bug-bitten back, chest, and arms. Her shoulders were slumped and she reminded him of a shell, kind of like a bleached-out June bug after the insides were gone.

After the funeral, his parents didn't pay much attention to George for a while. When the coroner had told them that Linden died of Rabbit Fever, he felt like they blamed him. Later he looked up Rabbit Fever in the library encyclopedia at school and found that it really did exist. The proper name was Tularemia and it was a disease caught from animals. Linden was always bringing home sick or injured animals. He had been scared of the woods though, and found his animals in the brush closer to the houses, or around the Papertown shacks.

George had always felt that Linden was a little bit of a sissy for being scared, and now he felt guilty for thinking that. He did love his little brother. George never mentioned any of this to anyone though. Now, he felt like he was very alone in the world.

Pete Rickson alternated between smoking Camels and Lucky Strikes and frequently had open packs of both in the house. George had taken a puff now and then from his friends when he was hanging around with the Hartwells. All of the boys, except George, smoked whenever they could get their hands on them. George hadn't cared much for it then, but now that he was alone, he decided to give it another try. His dad also kept a couple of Falstaff beers in their icebox and left the remainder of his six-pack under the edge of the back porch. George decided to try a beer too.

On a Friday afternoon when his mother was visiting a friend, He swapped a warmer bottle from under the porch with a cold one in the icebox, moving the other cold one to the front. He had been pilfering cigarettes one-at-a-time for a few days.

With his cigarettes and bottle of beer in hand, he settled in behind the outhouse, his back to the wall.

George was daydreaming, reminiscing about traveling with the *Young Hellion*s, with half of the beer gone, when his dad stepped around the corner of the outhouse. George knocked the bottle over as he jumped to his feet. He dropped the cigarette between his legs on the way up and tried to bury it with his shoe.

"Pick that up. NOW!" Pete thundered.

George looked down and saw beer sloshing from the top of the bottle. He grabbed it up while there was still some left. As he straightened up, Pete yanked the bottle from his hand and poured the rest over his son's head.

George was stunned speechless, and then Pete smacked him on the side of the head with the heel of his hand, knocking him down.

His father stood over him, his eyes blazing. "Don't you think I know a warm beer from a cold one?

"Don't you think I know how many I have? Or how many cigarettes?"

Did you think we were so blind that we couldn't see your smoke rising over the roof of this outhouse?"

Pete paused his rapid-fire rant, and then started in again. "If I ever catch you smoking again, no matter how old you are, I'll kick your ass up over your head. Most of all, most of all -he reiterated- Don't steal...You can drink when you are twenty-one." Then his shoulders slumped and he reached a hand down to his son, to pull him up.

"George, you're too old for me to be laying hands on you. I don't ever want to hit you again. Don't give me a reason too. Now go get cleaned up."

As they started towards the house, Pete grabbed his arm. "One other thing; stay away from that Coca-Cola stuff too. It's a habit-forming drug. Cocaine!"

After a month, George's mother came out of her shell to some extent and started paying some attention to her remaining son. One Saturday she drove him to town in the family car. George couldn't remember her driving before, but he wasn't surprised that she could. She took him to the movie theater for the Saturday Matinee. This was something she had done with Linden, but never with George.

On the occasions when she and Linden went to town, they had gone with a lady friend of his mother's named Margarite Wilkes, who picked them up in her own car. George really didn't like the woman and probably wouldn't have gone anyway, but he wasn't asked. He thought that he should have been, but never said anything to anyone about it. The woman had a black moustache and always wore bright red lipstick. She always grabbed the boys and tried to kiss them on the cheek, leaving a big red smear. Linden didn't seem to mind, but George avoided her most of the time. He couldn't stand the thought of being kissed by a moustache.

On this occasion it was just George and his mother. For twenty-five cents each, they got to watch two movies and several cartoons. George got the most kick out of the *Woody Woodpecker* cartoons. He had heard of the movies and read both of the books, which were *Tarzan and the She-Devil* and *20,000 Leagues Under the Sea*. In the Tarzan movie, he could tell that his mom really liked Raymond Burr, who played the bad guy. George liked Joyce MacKenzie, who played Jane, but he thought the part where she tangled with the crocodile and the snake was too phony. The Twenty-Thousand Leagues movie was his favorite of the two even though it didn't match the book in some places. He would have watched them both again, especially this one. He had read all of the Jules Verne books and most of the Edgar Rice Burroughs books too.

When they left the theater, it was late afternoon and the town seemed full. George was surprised to walk out into bright sunlight after being in the darkened theater. His mom took him to the Sugar Plum restaurant where he ordered a cheeseburger deluxe. It came with lettuce, tomatoes, mayonnaise, pickles and onions. He added his own ketchup and mustard. For a side item, he ordered french fries. His mom had an open-faced roast turkey sandwich with sweet potatoes and green beans. They were able to sit by the front window of the restaurant.

The sidewalks were full of people who came to town on Saturday night, even though it wasn't yet dark. Some stood alone and some in small groups on the corners and in front of the stores. A few were actually shopping from store-to-store, but most were either socializing or just watching others as they passed by. There was a continuous flow of cars passing by but no one seemed to be in a hurry. People would step into the street to cross it or to talk with people in the cars. There was a lot of honking and waving as the traffic all had to stop and go in unison, but no one seemed upset.

George noticed that people seemed to congregate by either social or age-related status, mostly age-related. His mother pointed out various people for whatever reasons. Some she identified as parents of his classmates and others by community status. She even pointed out the town drunk, a man referred to as High Pockets because he staggered around with both hands tucked under the chest flap of his bib overalls.

The man was rail-thin and goggle-eyed, wearing a stained white dress shirt and dark-blue bib overalls. He had a railroad cap of the same blue, but with thin white stripes.

Pointing her finger at the man, his mom said, "High Pockets has a bottle under his bib."

George laughed as the man leaned back against a lamppost just then and pulled the bottle out for a drink. After he had sucked the last drops from the bottle, he left his support post and dropped it in the wire-mesh trash basket just outside the restaurant. He glanced up as he released the bottle and caught George staring through the window at him. George saw a fleeting haunted look in the bloodshot eyes and then the man jerked away from the stern gaze of George's mother.

George knew there was more to the man than just a bottle of whiskey. He didn't know how. He just knew. As they left the restaurant, he glanced into the trash basket at the bottle and noticed the label read "Wild Turkey Straight Bourbon Whiskey, One Pint." He wondered what the man's story might be.

Another town character caught his mother's eye. This one was a woman in her forties with long, artificial-looking black hair and course features. She was wearing pink lipstick and a faded, red party dress that belted at the waist with a broad, black, patent-leather belt. She was barefoot and also appeared to have been drinking. To George, she was dumpy looking in the dirty red dress she was wearing. The dirty feet with blackened nails made it even worse. She leered at both of them with an open mouth, exposing toothless gums.

George's mom grimaced, even though they couldn't hear what the woman was saying. Someone leaving the restaurant just then steered the woman away.

"Don't ever go near that woman. Her name is Mary Simmonds," his mother said disgustedly.

George didn't ask why. Actually, he'd already heard of her, but couldn't imagine doing it with her as some of the other boys claimed they had.

During their stay in the restaurant, and after they left, he was surprised at how many people knew his mother and would stop to talk with her. He felt both proud and embarrassed. He hadn't realized she was so well known, or so popular. Many offered condolences regarding Linden. She accepted them graciously and always managed to steer the conversation to something else.

George had plenty of opportunity to look at other kids although there weren't that many near his age, and none that he knew on the sidewalks.

He heard his name called and looked out into the street. There was his friend Ollie, beckoning him from the passenger window of a car. George didn't know the middle-aged woman driving, but it wasn't Ollie's mother.

He talked very briefly with Ollie, not knowing what to say about his paralysis. "Hey, call me when you get a nickel," Ollie said as they moved on. Now, George noticed other kids looking his way. There were other schools in the county, and kids he didn't know were looking him over.

He saw a number of younger kids in cars waiting for their parents to conduct whatever business they had. He and Linden had waited in the car many times themselves, but he could never remember doing it on a Saturday evening.

There were three taverns in the three-block stretch of downtown. Two were in one block and one in another. A display window in Pop's Tavern had several stuffed animals in different, unnatural looking poses. To George, they looked old and moth-eaten.

A bank and a Sears' store took up most of the center block. The Sugar Plum Restaurant was in this block and the theater was opposite the restaurant. A drug store stood on every corner.

George noticed that there were cars parked on both sides of the streets in front of the taverns with kids in them. He knew some of these kids would have to wait for hours without being able to use a toilet.

His mom noticed him looking and, as if reading his mind, said, "Those poor kids. The parents should be horse-whipped." George was surprised at the vehemence in her voice.

George saw one other thing on this trip that really caught him off guard. He saw a bald-headed woman. If he had thought about it at all, he would have thought that only men would lose their hair. This woman looked about sixty. She was totally bald on top of her head, down to about an inch above her ears. From there she had thin, gray-white hair falling nearly to her shoulders. Her sunburned ears stuck out through the thin hair and were scabbed and peeling. The top of her head was tanned. George tore his eyes away as his mom pulled on his arm. He sneaked one more peek. He felt sorry for the woman but wondered why she didn't wear a hat or bonnet.

"Come on, she wants you to look at her," his mother said. George didn't ask why.

CHAPTER 8

One Friday of the next spring, Henry McDews, the older of Annie's two remaining kids, approached George after school and asked if he wanted to come over to their house after supper and "play some cards." Henry had grown some and looked almost identical to his older brother, Ralphie.

George was surprised but said, "Sure." He was even more surprised that there was a deck of cards anywhere in Papertown, and even more yet that they were the ones who had them. George's parents owned cards but only got them out when they had company or relatives over in the winter. The kids would play with the cards during the day and the men would play with them at night.

After supper that evening, he left the house without saying anything, which wasn't unusual. He went over to the back of the Corbett house and up the outside stairway, noticing the Corbett's Cadillac was gone. It was hot, and only the upstairs screen door was closed. This house was the only place around that had screen doors.

Annie was waiting for him and held the door open, forcing him to brush against her as he entered.

"Bet you're wanting to know where we got the cards," she said. "Henry and Connie found them behind a baseboard in the big room. I figure Mr. Corbett hid them from his Mrs. I don't know who he was playing with though, unless it was himself," she giggled. George thought back and recalled that the Corbetts had three grown daughters. All three had left for parts unknown as soon as they left school. He had heard a rumor that one of them was in California, but no one had much to say about them. He assumed that the girls had shared the upstairs with Mrs. Corbett's mother, who had passed away four or five years back.

Annie was proud of her accommodations and gave George a quick peek at each of the rooms. The upstairs contained three main rooms. The big room was in the center, with a small, enclosed sink at the front of the house, just under a small window looking out onto the street below. A small corner room on the same end held a commode and a bathtub. The commode was cracked and dry and a wadded-up towel was stuffed into its throat.

A doorway on the opposite side concealed an inside stairway that led down into the main house. Furniture in the big room was an old, wide-armed, gray sofa with and end table at each end, a plain rectangular wooden table, and four mismatched kitchen chairs.

The two bedrooms were on either side, under the sloping roofline. One of them held two twin beds, which looked to George like two halves of a bunk bed, and a single nightstand between them with a brown plastic radio on it. The other bedroom, obviously Annie's, had a larger daybed and a small dressing table. Each bedroom had a closet at one end and a small dormer window at one side. He knew that one of them looked down onto his own house.

The closets also had a small door opening into the big room at the stairway end, allowing entrance or pass-through in either direction. There was a single ceiling light in the big room, closer to the street end. The rest of the lighting was by table lamps.

George and Annie played war with the kids and tried a couple of other games they didn't really know how to play. Annie told George that the Corbetts had gone to a Pentecostal-sponsored tent revival about fifty miles away and they would be gone until *real* late.

Having drunk several glasses of lemonade, Connie, the youngest needed to go to the outhouse. By now it was after dark and Annie made Henry walk her out there and back. They weren't worried about animals, but about the men in Papertown. While they were gone, Annie gave George a passionate kiss and squeezed his upper thigh. George was flooded with desire and wanted more.

She pushed him away and said, "After the kids go to sleep, we'll go to my room."

He could hardly keep his composure when the younger kids came back. They played cards a while longer, then the kids wanted to listen to their radio programs. They liked *Fibber McGee and Molly, The Lone Ranger, Amos and Andy* and others including *The Shadow*.

George and Annie played cards, including a game called Hearts, at the small kitchen table while the kids listened to the radio in their bedroom. After what seemed like hours to George, she quietly turned down the radio and checked to make sure the kids were sleeping. Holding her finger to her lips, she took him by the hand, closed the door, and led him to her bedroom. "If one of the kids wakes up, sneak out through the closet," she whispered.

Each was frantic for both sex and attention. They whispered and held each other between bouts of lovemaking and then started again. He learned things he hadn't even heard of and things he wouldn't have believed was possible for two people to do. While holding her tight he asked if other people did the things they were doing.

"I don't know what all other people do when they're alone, but I know they do most of what we're doing and probably things we ain't thought of yet," she said.

George lay there on his back beside her awhile with his arms above his head to expand his lungs. Crazy thoughts raced through his mind and he finally said, "I saw Corbett up here with you more than once."

Annie turned toward him and laid a hand on his chest. "George, I have two kids to take care of and without this job I would be destitute. Sure, I let him feel me up some now and then. It don't hurt none, and I'm not going to let him get me in a predicament where we'll be completely alone."

George lay there without speaking.

"Don't be jealous, George," she whispered into his ear.

He turned on his side, facing her, and whispered back, "I understand, but I don't have to like it."

They kissed without speaking again and then resumed their earlier positions on their backs. Still, George wondered.

Later, he awoke with a feeling of suffocation and one arm asleep. Annie was laying totally naked sprawled on top of him with her head over his shoulder and her breath blowing on the side of his face. He shifted under her trying to get out and she awoke with a start.

"Oh my God," she whispered, "you've got to get out of here. "Please be quiet."

Before he could say anything, she covered his mouth with hers. He could taste both of them in the kiss. He eased out of the bed and into his pants and shoes. Pulling his shirt on and fastening it with only a couple of buttons, he eased out the screen door, closing it gently behind him.

He was halfway down the stairs when the light came on.

The stairway steps passed just below the corner of the Corbett's kitchen window and George was framed in the light like a bug pinned to the wall. He and Mrs. Corbett stared at each other eye-to-eye, no more than four feet apart. She was standing at a sink with a glass in her hand. Behind her, Mr. Corbett was standing in the doorway with his hand still on the light switch.

George saw her mouth fly open and he jumped the remaining steps to the bottom, not knowing what might have come out of her mouth. He fell and rolled to his feet and ran through Papertown, stumbling over a sleeping dog in his flight. He watched from the edge of the woods until almost daylight, but no lights had come on in his own house.

He was in bed when his parents got up. He thought sure the Corbetts would be there shortly, but they never came.

The next afternoon a panel truck backed up to the bottom of the stairs below Annie's apartment and within an hour, the McDews were gone.

CHAPTER 9

A few days after Annie and her kids disappeared; George was walking along the mostly-deserted road toward Hastings' Store & Station. The day was unusually hot and still, and every step off the pavement raised a puff of dust. George was wearing bib overalls. He had taken his blue and white, horizontal-striped polo shirt off and tucked it into one side of the pants. He wasn't thinking about much of anything except having to lug the groceries back home.

A scattering of houses stood near the intersection where the store was located, but he hadn't reached the first of them yet. The first sound he was aware of was a hissing from the sand behind him. As he recognized the sound of an automobile tire in sand, he also heard the faint noise of weed tops ticking against the bumper and knew the car was nearly on top of him.

Without looking back, he dived into the small muddy ditch a few feet to his right, belly-flopping into the mud. He got a face full of it for his trouble, and came up wet and dripping, only to see the Corbetts' Cadillac rolling to a stop just beyond where he'd been walking. As he slogged back out of the mud and weeds to the dusty shoulder, Mr. Corbett rounded the back of the Cadillac and stalked toward him.

"Well boy, you pert-near got killed there. If I'd been going a bit faster you would of." George was still out of breath. His heart was pounding and he had nothing to say anyway.

Corbett continued, "You know you cost me a great deal boy. I had a good bit invested in that little hussy and not just money. You caused me to lose it all. If your daddy wasn't who he is, I'd take you down right here and now. As it is, you had better watch your back from here on out, and plan on leaving the area as soon as you're able. Stay out of my sight, too."

George was both scared and mad. He wished he could bust Corbett up-side the head with something. There wasn't anything there to use and he knew in the back of his mind that he wouldn't have tried it anyway. Mr. Corbett was a good-sized grown man who'd bossed rough crews for a long time.

Corbett turned, threw down his filterless Pall Mall cigarette, walked back to his car, and pulled smoothly back onto the road as though nothing had happened.

George knew that Corbett would have run him over if he hadn't jumped when he did. Not a single car had gone by during the entire episode. He wiped the mud from his face and hands, checked for traffic and then grabbed up the still burning cigarette. He took a deep drag, choked on it, and threw it back down.

Mud and weeds had gone down the front of his overalls, too. He dropped his pants to the ground to clean off his chest and belly. He also checked for leeches. He used the shirt to wipe himself down and then brushed mud and dust from his clothes as best he could. He picked off a few sandburs too.

Hastings had an outside pump and he knew he'd have to wet his shirt to get his face and hands clean before going into the store. Dirty clothes were normal for the area, but he had to be wearing the shirt to go into the store. As he started to continue his trek, he glanced down to where the tracks left the road and then continued back onto the pavement. He walked beside them and noticed Corbett's footprints. There was a lump in the sand beside the wheel track near where the footprints began and ended.

He recognized the lump as a dust-covered wallet and picked it up from the sand. It was Eugene Corbett's wallet and held over four hundred dollars in cash along with his drivers' license and other papers. He looked around and saw there was still no one in sight.

He ran across the road to the brush-grown fence line and broke off a sapling with leaves. Returning, he hurriedly brushed out the footprints he'd made along with Corbett's footprints, the tire tracks, and the place where he'd found the wallet. He backtracked, walking backwards in his own tracks, brushing them out behind him so that there was no trail from the ditch to the pavement. He put out the cigarette and threw it across the road, then ran back down the pavement the way he'd come for about fifty yards and crossed the road to the other side where there was no ditch.

He found a spot near a broken-off tree and hid the wallet under the downed treetop. He removed all traces of this and ran back up the pavement well past the place where he had nearly been run over. He didn't stop running until he was out of breath. His plan was to run across the ditch and into the woods if he saw Corbett coming back. No one could find him in the woods.

He thought of the rifle and wished he'd had it. A second thought and he knew he was better off not having it. He would be fifteen in a few days and his dad had given him a "Ranger" single-shot, bolt-action .22 caliber rifle. The rifle had a solid barrel and receiver with a round cocking knob at the breech. George could hit a squirrel in the head with this rifle nearly every time.

He had been putting meat on the table by sneaking into barns and shooting pigeons with a Daisy pump BB gun. He only kept the breasts, and his parents never saw them before George cleaned them. He told them they were doves. His mother didn't like him killing the *doves,* but she wouldn't have tolerated pigeons. The meat was tasty and she ate it too.

Old man James had shown him how to clean them by jamming a thumb into the bird's belly below the ribs. It didn't require much effort to reach up under the ribs and tear them away with the breast meat attached. He easily tore the patch of skin and feathers off and discarded it with the rest of the animal. The procedure was messy but efficient.

Pete Rickson gave him the rifle was so he could kill off any rabbits in the area and bring in squirrels for the table. Rabbits were not on the menu since Linden died. His dad just wanted them killed.

"Kill them all Son, and leave them lay. They're nothing but disease-bearing, long-eared rats. They don't do the world a bit of good."

George made it all the way to Hastings and back without seeing a trace of Corbett. He waited three days before retrieving the wallet on a moonlit night.

Over the next couple of weeks, he spent several late afternoons in the woods just on the other side of Papertown, watching the Jompson shack. Most afternoons Deeter came home in the car with other workers and talked with them for a while before heading for his shack. This gave George plenty of time for part of what he wanted. The other part was to catch Molly gone from the shack when Deeter got there.

He finally got his chance one afternoon when Molly got tired of waiting for Deeter to stop yakking, and headed for the outhouse. As soon as George was sure she was gone, and Deeter had stepped out of his buddy's car but was still talking, he slipped around the corner of their shack from the far side and pitched Mr. Corbett's wallet into the shack and onto the floor where Deeter couldn't miss it. He had previously removed over three hundred dollars of the money, wrapped it in several layers of waxed paper, and stashed it in a hiding place under his house. Even if he ever left home, he could still get at it. He thought that some day, some way, he would find Annie and get the money to her.

From the back of the shack, George wasn't disappointed. He stuck around just long enough to hear Deeter say, "What the hell!" and then grunt.

George circled around all the shacks and eased onto the back-porch steps of his own house, whittling on a stick and waiting to see what would happen next. When Molly got back, Deeter flattened her with one punch, knocking her out of the shack into the dirt. He kicked her in the ribs and butt until she started crying and crawled away on her hands and knees with Deeter following along, calling her whore and money-grubbing slut. Their neighbors were used to it and didn't interfere.

An hour later Deeter caught up with Corbett as he was getting out of his Cadillac. "Lose something Corbett?" Deeter said as he pitched the wallet up on top of the car.

Corbett grabbed the wallet. "Where'd you get this Jompson?" Then, as he noticed all the cash was missing, "You stole my money!"

Deeter's work boot caught him square in the crotch and then in the face as he doubled over. Trapped between the open door and the car, Corbett couldn't even roll away. He dropped to his knees with blood pouring from his nose and mouth. Though Deeter was smaller, he grabbed Corbett by the hair and dragged him to the back of the car and threw him face down into the dirt.

"I'll teach you not to mess with what's not yours you big-shot son of a bitch!"

He kicked Corbett repeatedly in the head and back, and rabbit-punched him on the back of the neck until several people who had been cheering him on finally stopped talking and pulled him off. He stumbled away in a daze and Mr. Corbett lay there as if dead.

That night Deeter Jompson went to jail and then, later on, to the state prison, not to be seen for a long time to come.

Both Molly and Mr. Corbett went to the hospital. Molly returned with a black eye, one cheek puffed out as if she had half a baseball in it, and blackened blood on a split lip. The next day she begged Mrs. Corbett to let her stay, claiming no knowledge of why Deeter had attacked her husband or Molly, herself.

"You know there are vicious people around here who hate us, and they would do anything to get rid of us," she appealed.

Mrs. Corbett looked to the heavens for inspiration just as the preacher drove up in his 49 Plymouth. Molly got a reprieve and later she wound up paying her way by caring for Mr. Corbett when he returned from the hospital a week later. He had suffered a stroke and never walked again. He wasn't even able to roll his own wheelchair.

Mrs. Corbett continued to run Papertown, but sporadically. When she was paying attention, it was with an iron fist. When she wasn't, it was because of time she spent praying and bible studying with the, younger than her, widower preacher. The preacher began spending more time at the Corbetts' house and when he was there, Mrs. Corbett began sending Molly away.

Molly claimed they were doing stuff right in front of Mr. Corbett, who couldn't even talk. "He knows though," Molly said. "He drools more and shakes on one side. Some of the time when the preacher is there, he and Mrs. Corbett are in the upstairs apartment where Annie McDews and her kids lived. Mr. Corbett rolls his eyes up toward the ceiling."

CHAPTER 10

Less than two months later, Molly spotted George sitting on his back-porch steps one morning. She beckoned him to follow her to the back of Papertown, toward where the farthest community outhouse was. George noticed that her face had healed, leaving only a thin scar at one corner of her mouth.

He thought she wanted to ask him something about the Corbetts or needed help with something. It was too early in the morning to holler back and forth so he followed her and was surprised when she continued to the edge of the woods. She suddenly disappeared completely and George went on a ways to find her sitting on the ground behind a scrub pine about four feet tall. The area just outside the woods was dotted with them.

She motioned him to sit down with her and he did. She said, "Missing little Annie, George?"

George blushed and stammered, "She was just a friend."

She reached over and touched him on the cheek. "It's Okay baby, I know what you were doing and I got something better'n she's got."

She opened the top of her gray, button-down dress, reached in, and pulled a big white breast out into the open. The nipple was as big as George's middle fingertip and the dark-pink areola around it was as big around as a coffee cup. He could see veins under the dusty white skin and long, dark curly hair under her arms.

She laughed at his expression and said, "What's the matter big boy, cat got your tongue?" Before he could say anything, she said, "Get that bird out. I want what she was gettin."

She reached up under her dress from the bottom and pulled out a folded-up, thin, dingy-looking blanket. She spread it out beside her and rolled onto it on her back with her knees in the air, and pulled the front of the dress up to her waist. She was wearing nothing under it.

George knew what to do—and did it. Even as he was crawling on top of her, he couldn't believe they were out in the open in broad daylight. All anyone would have to do was walk a hundred feet past the outhouse to see them.

Before he could finish, her smell grew so strong he almost pulled away from her. His hesitation only seemed to goad her on as she locked her legs around him and pulled his head down to the still exposed breast.

"Suck on that," she cried, "you won't get a better one."

George did his best though the nipple was stiff and crusty and he thought wildly about biting it off. She gave a huge, heavy moan and quivered, smothering his face between her breasts.

Before he knew it, she was pushing him off saying, "You've got stayin power boy. We'll do it again."

In another minute, she had folded up the blanket, tucked it up under her dress, and was gone. The smell of her hung in the air like an invisible fog and he became nauseous and stumbled toward the woods, still pulling up his pants.

He tried to avoid her for a while, but within two weeks she motioned to him again from the edge of the shacks. The lust for her raw sex almost made him dizzy when he thought about it. She disappeared into her shack and was out in a minute with a triumphant grin. He could tell she was holding her blanket up under her dress.

They met again a few more times. Each time her musk seemed to grow even stronger. Finally, the time came when he couldn't finish and couldn't satisfy her. He rolled away and dry heaved into the weeds.

She jumped up and kicked him in the side with her bare foot. "I thought you was a man, you little prick. I'll find somebody else to do the job." She kicked him once more and left.

He was glad it was over. A week later she packed her clothes, walked to the highway, and lifted her skirt to a big car with two men in it. She never came back and he never saw her again.

CHAPTER 11

The rest of that summer George spent a lot of time alone in the woods behind his house and Papertown. Sometimes he hunted young groundhogs for meat or just plinked at cans, bottles and rabbits dumb enough to sit in the afternoon sun. Sometimes he spent days just watching the animals, birds and bugs and never fired a shot.

One day, as he was walking down the road, Dean pulled up beside him in his car. "Howdy George, Whatcha doin with that rifle?"

"I thought I might pop a squirrel or two," George replied.

"Get in, I'm going to try out a rifle myself and I've got a place a couple miles from here."

He got in and Dean drove to a place George had never been to before. They parked at the edge of the woods and then went plinking along through the brush and trees, shooting at tin cans, sparrows, mushrooms and knotholes. Dean had a Remington model 550-1 .22 semi-automatic rifle, but couldn't seem to get it to shoot where he wanted it too. They switched rifles and tried a few shots. George couldn't hit anything with it either, but Dean could hit everything he shot at with George's rifle.

George took a sighting along Dean's rifle barrel. "Hell Dean, your barrel is bent!"

Dean took a sighting too, then threw it down. "That damned crook. I bought this at the sporting goods store. I'm taking it back."

They meandered back through the woods, taking turns with George's rifle. After a while, they stopped for a few minutes and took a break. Dean fired up a cigarette and they just sat on a log and talked. During a lull in the conversation, a large, fully-grown groundhog came rustling up through the leaves. It didn't seem to notice them when they first heard it. Then it stopped and sat straight up right in front of George's rifle barrel. Without conscious thought, George slid the safety off and pulled the trigger. The groundhog flipped over onto its back, rolled over and scurried away.

George was so surprised that the long-rifle shot in the throat hadn't killed it, that he just sat there for a few seconds. Dean jumped up and ran after it with his bent rifle, firing as he ran. He caught up with it and kept firing right down into it. The groundhog slowed and then began climbing a small blasted-off tree trunk. Dean fired twice more and ran out of bullets.

The groundhog made it about six feet up the tree, nearly to its splintered top, before George caught up with them. He dispatched it with one shot to the base of its skull. As it fell, both boys slumped over in exhaustion.

"My God," Dean gasped, "I must have shot it twenty times."

"I know. I can't believe how tough it was."

"And I didn't know they could climb trees," Dean said.

After dropping George off where he found him, Dean took the groundhog home to skin it, count the bullet holes, and eat it. George never did find out how many shots it had taken, or what happened to the bent-barreled rifle. He wondered why he had even shot the ground hog to start with.

Sometimes George sat in the woods just thinking about random things. Sometimes he thought about what life might be like in other places.

He had a soldier uncle who had been to Korea, fought in a war, and was going back. The uncle had a friend killed right beside him over there.

George thought about life and death. He also thought about stories he read in the library books at school or stories the teachers told of their lives. There was an English teacher named Mrs. Cobberly, who he really liked. She had encouraged him to read many different kinds of books. He always got an "A" in her classes. She told him the books would help him seek out better places and a better life. He tried to imagine how different life would be in a big city or in a different country. He liked stories about the settling of America and life in the West, especially California.

His uncle, Ward Rickson, looked nothing like his brother, George's dad. Ward was short and stocky with dark red hair, twinkling blue eyes and an easy grin. George got his height, wiry dark hair, and dark eyes from his father. His classic features and clear-smooth complexion, he got from his mother.

Ward was only five years older than George and acted like a big brother when he was around, talking to him in confidence like a grown man. He told dirty jokes and stories George knew his parents wouldn't want him to hear. When Ward came back from his basic training, and before his tour in Korea, he wrestled with George who was taller, and showed George the hand-to-hand combat moves he'd learned. Most of it was a form of Judo and Jujitsu using leverage and the opponents own body weight against him.

George found a book on Jujitsu in the library at school and was able to make the rough sessions with Ward more interesting. Once George's dad saw them scuffling and had a talk with both of them about self-defense. He had been a boxer in the Army during World War II and had been successful enough to be a division light-heavyweight champion. He was convinced that boxing was the best hand-to-hand defense skill, but told them they needed to learn other methods of fighting so they could counter whatever attack came their way.

He did say, "If the opponent is more skilled than you, use something else. Box a wrestler, wrestle a boxer." He told them how being in the ring once saved his life. While in the Philippines at the end of the war, he was giving an impromptu exhibition for the natives and sparring with a heavyweight. The hutch he would normally have been in at the time was blown up with a grenade, killing two of his squad.

Months later, Ward returned from Advanced Infantry Training with a whole new set of skills including the use of nerves and pressure points and how to kill a man in several ways by breaking his neck, choking, or stabbing him. By this time, Ward had been in a number of big-city military bar brawls and his nose was no longer quite straight. He showed George a few things about hurting a man without killing him and cautioned him to avoid trouble with Army paratroopers or Navy frogmen. Now Ward was gone again, back to Korea.

CHAPTER 12

During that summer, four young girls disappeared from the county in which George lived. Their ages ranged from seven to twelve. George knew nothing of this until the Sheriff's department showed up in Papertown, questioning all the adults. George asked one of the Papertown kids what was going on when he saw the brown and tan car with the star on the side. No one seemed to know anything about the missing girls, except that two of them were missing from Papertown. George remembered years back, thinking Fowler McDews had been taking kids. Now he was not so sure. He knew that McDews had been bad all the way through though, and too keep his mouth shut about it.

Summer turned to fall and George returned to school and hunting for meat with his Ranger rifle during afternoons and weekends. George also fell in love.

Her name was Carrie Epps and she was pretty, with blue eyes and honey-blonde hair. Carrie was fifteen and in the same class as George. Her parents had been killed in a car crash and she had moved in with an aunt and uncle, Florence and Elmer Johnson. Her uncle sold insurance in the local area.

Carrie's looks and status, as well as her self-isolation, kept her apart from others her age.

A chance meeting in the library attracted her to George who stayed apart from others of his own accord. He didn't ignore her, but didn't pursue her either. Later she told him she liked that he didn't put on airs or talk dirty in front of her like the other boys. She was surprised that he had actually read some of the books she was looking at.

She lived only a short distance beyond where George lived and when he found this out, he began circling back to the road from his hunting trips so that he came out beyond her house. Before long, she stopped him to talk while she was on her front porch swing as he came by.

The aunt, a shapeless gray-haired woman with coke-bottle thick glasses, was an alcoholic who pretty much ignored her and had only taken her in because she was a brother's daughter.

Carrie began taking walks of her own and sometimes was waiting when George came out of the woods. She told him of missing life in town and all the friends she had to leave behind, mentioning boy's names to see his reaction. She saw he was interested, but didn't really want to hear about the boys.

One Saturday morning she surprised him by showing up at the edge of the woods past her house, catching him where he emerged before reaching the road. Her hair was in a single, thick braid down her back to the waist, and she was wearing a white blouse and sneakers with pink shorts ending a few inches above the knee. George hadn't seen girls his age wearing shorts and none with their legs exposed above the knee. If it were anyone else, he would have thought of her as a tramp. Instead, he thought maybe that's how girls in town dressed.

He could see her brassiere through the white blouse and was surprised to see she had breasts as large as a grown woman's. They were as big as Molly's, but didn't appear to sag. He noticed a briar scratch on her leg and thought about licking the single drop of blood, then forced the thought from his head.

It dawned on him that Carrie was talking to him about hunting and asking him to show her how. He already had two squirrels in the old flour bag, the open end of which was tucked into one side of his belt, but he agreed to try for one more squirrel. He cautioned her to silence as he took her by the hand and led off at a tangent to an area of white oaks he hadn't previously hunted.

As they wound through the woods avoiding the thickets, he heard a strange sound, almost a whimper. He squeezed Carrie's hand tightly and then released it so he could lower his rifle from his shoulder. They both heard the whimpering sound again and looked at each other as if for confirmation. Then they heard a smack and a man's voice.

"Shut up you little bitch or I'll be hurtin you worse."

George and Carrie crouched down and eased forward on hands and knees. As they drew closer, they heard grunting, leaves rustling, and then the whimpering again. What they saw in the next minute shocked them both.

A grown man was on top of a little girl with his knees on the ground and his pants bunched down around them, his bare ass thrusting at her. He had one hand on her throat and the other raised to strike her again. The girl, about nine, was on her back and naked from the waist down. Both her face, and what they could see of her thigh from one side, were bloodied. George sensed motion at his side and saw Carrie starting to rise. He could tell by her face that she was going to scream or cry out. He grabbed her arm and pulled her back down, pointing to his rifle. She nodded as if she understood what he was going to do, before he was sure himself.

George whispered, "I know the man. It's Edgar Semms from Papertown. I don't know the girl. I'm going to shoot him in the foot so he can't run away. The girl will probably run, so you'll have to catch her."

Carrie's eyes were as big as saucers. She nodded and whispered, "Hurry."

George took careful aim so he wouldn't hit the girl during her struggles. Semms was moving but his feet were planted in his effort to keep her from wriggling out from under him. George shot him right at the bony protrusion at the top of his work shoe. Carrie, Semms, and the little girl all screamed at the sound of the shot.

Carrie hollered "Run" as loud as she could. Semms rolled to the far side to use the girl as a shield, but lost his grip on her throat. She scrambled away from him and ran blindly, in a half crouch. Carrie ran after her as George kept his rifle lined up on Semms while he worked the bolt and loaded another long-rifle shell into the chamber.

Semms was hollering, "Who is it? Jesus, you broke my foot, come on, we can work something out." He was trying to crawl behind a bush while he hollered.

George let him get almost behind it and then shot him in the anklebone on the other foot.

Semms screamed again and hollered, "Oh God! Oh God! Oh God!"

George wanted to finish him off, but knew he would be in big trouble if he did. He wished now that Carrie hadn't been with him. Satisfied that Semms wouldn't be going far, he scrambled away and listened for sounds of Carrie and the girl. Trotting through the woods in the direction they had gone, he finally heard them and hollered, "Carrie it's me, it's OK, it's OK!"

Carrie had the girl pressed against her to cover her as best she could. The bottom half of her dress was completely gone. George turned his back, took his shirt off and handed it back to Carrie. She tied it around the child like an apron and took her hand to lead her away. The girl seemed frightened of George and kept hiding behind Carrie. Her eyes seemed to be darting in all directions at once and she kept glancing over her shoulder as if expecting to see her attacker following behind her.

Carrie said, "It's Okay honey. He can't ever hurt you again."

They took the girl to Carrie's house and arrived just as her uncle drove into the driveway in his Straight-Eight Pontiac. This was the first time George had seen the uncle. He was a plump, completely bald man with wire-framed glasses. George had never seen a man dressed as he was. He was wearing pastel green slacks over ox-blood penny-loafers, with a yellow button-down shirt. A green and brown paisley tie hung from his neck with the knot pulled loose.

While George was gawking at him, it finally sunk in that the man was demanding to know what was going on before he was completely out of the car. The shirtless, dirty George with his rifle and bloody bag hanging from his side was the focus of his demands. He made a grab for the rifle when he got close. George stepped back, holding the rifle across his chest with both hands.

"Sir, your niece is all right. Ask her."

The uncle glared at George, but listened as Carrie poured out what had happened in a rush of words. "What were you doing in the woods with him?" he asked.

"This girl's been raped and a man has been shot!" she screamed back at him.

This finally seemed to register with the uncle, and George took the opportunity to say, "I have to tell my Dad." He took off, running for home.

CHAPTER 13

George's parents were not at home when he got there. He had forgotten they had gone to the county seat to shop. He left his rifle in the house, grabbed a shirt, and ran over to the center of Papertown knowing that some men should be there.

He shouted. "Any men, come out! Any men come out!" Several men and a lot of women and kids came out of the shacks.

"What the hell's going on?" one of the men snarled." He was a burly, wiry-haired, sawyer who worked for Corbett's brother.

"There's been a crime," George said, "I have to talk to the men alone."

They could tell by his face that it was serious. A couple of men grabbed George by the shoulders and the burly sawyer who had snarled at him told all of the women and kids to go back into their shacks until they found out what was going on.

The men walked him to the end of the shacks and back behind the outhouse. The sawyer said, "All right, talk damn it!"

George looked around to see if Junior Semms was with them, but didn't see him. He told the men that he and a girl friend had caught Edgar Semms raping a little girl in the woods and that he'd shot Semms in both feet so he couldn't run away.

"I knew that worthless Semms was up to something," one of the men said.

"He probably took them girls that's been missing too," another said.

This got the attention of all of them. "OK boy. You show us where he's at," said the sawyer.

"Why didn't you shoot him in the head?" another asked.

"Because there were two girls there," George said.

They all were silent for a moment, looking at him.

"By God I believe you would have, boy," someone else said.

"If he had, we wouldn't be able to find out what else Semms has been up to," another said.

A couple of the men grabbed rifles and a couple more picked up clubs from their shacks as they left.

"Where's your rifle?" one of them asked George.

"In my house, where it'll stay," he said.

They gave him another odd look, but didn't push the matter.

"You'd better not be lying," the burly sawyer growled.

George led them through the woods for nearly half a mile to where they had found Semms and the girl. The men had all grown silent during the grim procession. There was a trail of bloody leaves leading away from the site.

"You stay right here with me," a man named Horace Jenkins said to George. Horace was a pleasant looking, average-sized man with sandy hair. He always appeared freshly shaven.

George was relieved not to be with the group of men whenever they found Edgar Semms. Within a few minutes someone shouted, "We found him. Take the kid home."

Horace Jenkins escorted George back to the road and then walked with him all the way home. Jenkins was one of the friendlier men in Papertown. He said, "You and I don't really want to know what's happening back there."

George had an idea, but it turned out that he was wrong.

CHAPTER 14

Horace stayed with George, sitting on the porch with him until his parents came home.

"Don't worry, George, I'll talk to your old man," he said.

He was as good as his word and took George's father off to the side before any questions started. George and his mother went inside and she began preparing a meal without speaking to him.

Shortly, his father came in and said, "Give me your rifle."

George handed it over, looking his father directly in the eye as he did. The return gaze was inscrutable. His father sat down at the table with some tools and proceeded to take the rifle apart. Finally, he took the firing pin out and laid it on the floor. With one blow of his hammer, he broke it into two pieces. He put the rifle back together without the firing pin, and handed it back to George.

"That's a good rifle and it's your property. When you're grown and on your own you can get another firing pin."

George picked up the pieces and put the rifle away without responding.

His father left soon after the meal saying, "Stay inside."

Without a word spoken from either of them, George and his mother took it to mean both of them. George glanced at her and suddenly realized she looked old, even though she wasn't. He put his arm around her and for the first time, the son was consoling the mother. Still, not a word was spoken.

His father returned within an hour. "No matter what happens or what we might hear, no one is leaving this house tonight. Mother, turn the radio on and turn it up so we can all hear it."

George fell asleep with the sound of gospel ringing in his ears. For once, he didn't try to sneak out at night. The next morning George's father was sitting at the table reading the newspaper when George woke up.

"Son, I'll walk you out back past the outhouse. The Sheriff is next door and he'll be by to ask you a few questions. Just answer the truth and nothing else. Got that? Just answer and tell him nothing else." When they were out of hearing range of the house, he said, "Oh, and just between you and me, you didn't have to shoot that man!"

"He would have killed me and Carrie too."

"Not likely! You would have gotten away. Not another word now; you hear me?"

George just nodded.

Later, the Sheriff arrived and asked George, "Why did you shoot him instead of holding him with the rifle?"

George noticed that the Sheriff had the broken pieces of his firing pin, rolling them around in his big hand as he talked. George had put the pieces up with his rifle, so his father must have given them to him.

George replied, "I was scared he would try to take the gun away, or use the girl to get it away from me."

"Since you shot him, why didn't you shoot to kill?"

"I didn't kill him because there were two girls there and I didn't want them to see that."

His father's face hardened. It might well have been carved from stone.

The Sheriff looked shocked and said "Son, you can't just kill a man because he done something bad. He has to go to court."

Neither George nor his father said another word. George still thought he should have killed Semms. He thought briefly about the rabbits, although his father never mentioned rabbits anymore. George had stopped killing them some time back. Rabbits didn't deliberately carry the disease that killed his little brother. It wasn't as if they would come into your house and bite you in your sleep like rats did. Semms was worse than a rat.

After another hour, Pete Rickson allowed George to leave the house. Papertown appeared completely deserted. Later, he found out from others what had happened.

The men had dragged and carried Edgar Semms back to Papertown. All of the women and kids of Papertown were loaded into the few cars available and were taken away to stay in a revival tent until the following evening.

After they were gone, the men beat Semms with clubs, burned him with cigarettes and cigars and pinched him with pliers. They twisted his shattered ankles until he confessed to killing the missing girls and told where they were left in the woods. They weren't done with him, but he got some respite while men with lanterns went to search for the bodies.

When word got back of the grizzly crime scenes, two men raised Semms upright. He couldn't stand on his own because of the broken and splintered ankles. They dragged him sobbing to the community clothesline made of separate, solid lines of number–nine galvanized wires stretched parallel about eighteen inches apart. They ducked under the first wire and then hooked his chin over the middle wire. Then, with several men pulling, they reached across from behind him and pulled the third wire over his head.

"That ought to hold you up," one said.

Another said. "Think about strangling those little girls."

With his eyes bulging out, Semms tried to turn his head to keep from being choked by the wire under his chin. Other men grabbed his hair and ears to hold his head straight. When they saw that he was about to choke to death, they kicked and pushed his legs out and up from behind, pushed up under his back, and flipped him completely over, putting a double twist in the wires.

His body hung up on the first wire for a moment, but his thrashing carried him past it. They had tied his hands behind him, but his legs were free and he danced a wild, tattoo *dance-of-death* as the men scrambled out of the way.

The bolted-together wooden crossties groaned and creaked, but they didn't break as he bounced back and forth. The wires screeched like an over-tuned fiddle.

They said he was still flopping and kicking like a chicken with its neck wrung when his bowels and bladder emptied. He slung urine and feces all over the surrounding area from his flopping pant legs. The sand under the clotheslines was torn up in a seven-foot circle.

Semmes's body hung there until the Sheriff came out the next morning. Searchers found a total of five girls' bodies in the woods near where George and Carrie had their encounter with him. No one was ever able to determine who the fifth girl was or where she came from.

Carrie's aunt and uncle took the girl George and Carrie rescued into town and left her at the city police station. From there, police took her to the hospital. George never heard who she was, or where she lived.

The Sheriff's report read simply, *Semms was killed by unknown persons while trying to escape.* When asked about it, he stated, "There will be no investigation into who actually killed him. That would be fruitless."

CHAPTER 15

That winter George's father got a letter from the Government stating that his brother, Ward Rickson, was *missing in action* in Korea.

Mrs. Corbett sold the home, business, and Papertown to a local farmer named Harold Schmidt who wanted to retire from farming and live off of income property.

George's dad said, "That will only last until he runs out of chickens."

Harold Schmidt was a short, rotund man with a balding fringe of dark hair who liked to wear suspenders over a dirty undershirt. He always started his day with a cap, but it invariably slid forward or backward on his bald crown and he eventually threw it aside until he left the area.

Harold swore a lot but was friendly and knew all of the surrounding farmers. He had done some mechanical work in the past and now took this up as well. He soon had a small business going, repairing farm equipment. Papertown kids were sent to adjacent farms to locate abandoned and junked equipment, taking handwritten notes to the farmers letting them know what kind of parts he needed. Before long, all of the previously unused space among the weeds around Papertown was strewn with farm equipment pieces.

George was soon helping him move heavier equipment and showed an aptitude for mechanical work. Once again, he had free access to Papertown.

It wasn't long after George started working with the farm equipment that Harold Schmidt taught him how to crank-start and drive the tractors. One was an F14 Farmall with a foot clutch. The other was a DC Case with a hand clutch, which made things confusing. Harold made him learn to operate the F14 for a month before he let him try the more powerful Case. Later he taught George how to back attached equipment and how to crank and start the old, 1928 *Diamond T* one-and-a-half-ton truck. George was impressed with how strong the truck was built, and how thick the metal was on the dark green fenders and black cab.

The truck had a six-volt battery under the floorboard on the passenger side, but most of the time the battery didn't have enough grunt to start the truck, and not at all in cold weather. The truck also had the gas tank under the seat, which reminded George of Fowler McDews.

He didn't think about that too often and always forced his thoughts to other things.

Now, he was learning from Harold Schmidt how to back a truck with a trailer, or a corn picker, attached to the frame-mounted drawbar using only the small round mirrors mounted on stalks on either side of the truck cab. George caught on but when he tried backing a four-wheeled wagon that way he could never get it to go where he wanted.

Schmidt saw him and had a good laugh, saying, "The hell, boy, I don't know anybody can do that."

George was working on a combine one Saturday when his parents were gone and Harold asked if he would like to have supper with them.

George said, "Sure." He really didn't know Mrs. Schmidt and hadn't exchanged more than hello's with her. He imagined she was a good enough cook though, from the girth of Harold.

The woman herself wasn't as "thin as a rail," as George's mother had once said. She hadn't meant it unkindly. The term was usually an inference that the person was a hard worker. Mrs. Schmidt wasn't as thin as George thought her to be, and she was actually shapely for an older woman. She had red hair with streaks of gray, a narrow full-lipped mouth and a twinkle in her pale blue eyes. Her eyes, nose, mouth and chipmunk-cheeks resided low on her face, below a high forehead.

George was looking forward to the meal as he had only eaten cold cornbread and beans for lunch. In his mind, he could already smell the meat cooking, hoping it was pork chops, his favorite. They seldom had them at home.

As the day wore on, the smell became real although some of it might have come from the homemade stoves in any of the shacks. He could hardly wait.

When they called him to supper, he brushed the dirt from his clothes and shoes before washing his hands and face at the washstand pump. When he entered the house, he could smell apple pie on top of other good aromas.

"Smells really good," he said.

Mrs. Schmidt patted him on the shoulder and pointed to a seat at one side of the rectangular table. She and Harold sat at opposite ends. Harold was already seated when he came in, but didn't have anything on his plate. George took the cue and waited for grace.

Mrs. Schmidt said a short blessing, then pointed to a large silver pot sitting on a cutting board in the middle of the table and said, "Help yourself, George, I know you'll like it. It's squirrel stew."

He was surprised because he had never seen it prepared this way. He remembered giving Harold some squirrels not long before. There was a bowl sitting on his plate and a ladle in the stew. The stew had a thin brown gravy texture and was loaded with potatoes, carrots, onions and celery along with the meat. When he brought the ladleful to the surface, he got another surprise. A grinning squirrel skull, complete with teeth, was staring at him. He nearly dropped the ladle before letting it back down into the pot.

Harold laughed. "What's the matter George, don't you like the head?"

George was embarrassed but he grinned and said, "I just like the legs better." He swirled the ladle around until he found something more to his liking.

Harold Schmidt fished around until he found a head. He set it on the side of his plate to drain and scooped out another. Then he loaded the rest of the plate with the potatoes and vegetables. He picked up a folded cloth from beside his plate, draped it over a squirrel head, and picked it up in his left hand. With his right hand, he smacked the covered skull lengthways with the edge of his fork.

"Don't want it to get away," he said.

He unwrapped the now-split skull, pried it apart, and proceeded to pick the brains out with the tines of his fork.

George noticed that he had a cloth beside his plate too, but he looked away and concentrated on his own meal. The food was excellent with separate plates and bowls of biscuits, mashed potatoes, milk-gravy, string beans and corn. The stew was also good once he got used to the idea of the heads being in there. He noticed Mrs. Schmidt didn't eat any of the heads either. Harold had them all to himself.

They had coffee with the pie and at first, George refused.

"You just don't know how to make it taste good," Harold said. He laced George's cup of coffee with cream and sugar until it was a khaki color.

George thought it really was good, a lot better than the bitter brew his parents drank. The apple pie turned out to be as good as everything else. George didn't understand how Mrs. Schmidt could be so slender and shapely with all that food around.

After the meal Harold Schmidt said, "I have something to show you George. Come on in here."

He led the way into the living room and pointed to a dark-colored, square television with a rounded-corner screen. It looked out of place sitting on a beautiful, mahogany, claw foot, sideboard buffet along the wall between two windows. The four long spindly legs of the sideboard looked as if they could barely support the weight. It was the first *TV* George had ever seen, having only seen photos of them in newspaper and magazine ads.

Harold twisted a dial to turn it on, and after what seemed like a long time, it gradually lit up with a loud hissing noise. All George saw were thousands of dancing black and white spots. While they were waiting, Harold said, "It's a stand-alone set but Mother didn't want to give up her sideboard, so I unscrewed the legs and set it up on top. It's a used one and it had a good picture in the store.

"I need to put up an antenna and I'll need your help. Are you doing anything tomorrow?"

"Not on Sunday, you can't work on Sunday, Harold." Mrs. Schmidt said.

"This is a hobby for me, not work," he replied.

"It sounds like fun to me," George said.

She threw up her hands and left the room. The next day they put up the antenna, attaching the pipe mount to the railing of the outside stairway, the same stairway George had been seen on by the previous owners. They extended the pipe high enough that the antenna barely cleared the peak of the roof. It took more time to get it adjusted in the best direction than it did to install the antenna and run the flat, brown, twin-lead wire. At first, they only had two channels that looked like targets and one of a flickering Indian head.

Harold had picked up some of the lingo at the appliance store. He told George that they were test patterns and the spots were called snow. They kept trying and found one station with a man talking about stomach acid while pointing at a blackboard with a stick, and another with a man dressed up in a cowboy outfit, playing a guitar and singing. They settled on this and watched *Bob Atcher, The Singing Cowboy*, followed by *Howdy Doody*.

"The hell, I was beginning to think we weren't going to get anything," Schmidt said.

A couple weeks later, his parents allowed George to stay home from school so he could watch the January 1953 inauguration of President Eisenhower at the Schmidt house. It was the first televised inauguration of a president. George was surprised at how many people were in the streets in cold weather. He thought most of it was pretty boring.

It wouldn't be long before he would forget his boredom.

CHAPTER 16

Junior Semms had quit school and worked in the sawmill for Corbett's brother. He had been there several months and was at work on the day they captured his dad for raping and killing the young girls. Word spread fast and, wisely, he stayed away for a few days. The other Papertown residents were indifferent to the rest of the Semms family and didn't seem to care whether they stayed or not. Despite his meanness, Junior was a hard worker and managed to keep his job.

The Papertown men ignored Junior and he avoided them when he wasn't working. Instead, he stayed with his younger brother and sisters when they were outside. When there were no adults around, he still bullied his siblings and other kids who got too close.

He was as mean as Robert Williams had been but was sneakier about it, seldom letting anyone but the smaller kids see his petty meanness. He had gained weight and muscle from working in the mill and had his black hair styled in a flattop, giving him a tough-guy look. At seventeen, he had a cocky, sneering attitude around the smaller kids. Sometimes he went out drinking with the young, hard-cases from the mill, who didn't live in Papertown.

One day when George was looking through the weeds around the edges of the shacks for a corn-picker part, a fist-sized rock whizzed past his head and thudded off a building behind him. He ducked and turned to find Junior Semms glaring at him.

"I've been waiting for a chance to clean your clock, Rickson. You interfered in my life too many times to get by with it. You should have minded your own business."

George didn't answer and was looking around for a weapon, assuming Junior had already pulled his knife.

"Well come on, George, I ain't got nothin and don't need nothin' to kick your ass."

As big as George was, Semms was two inches taller and twenty or more pounds heavier. He looked as mean as he was, with a raw-boned face, thick eyebrows and a two-day beard stubble. He had broad shoulders and long arms to go with the look.

A few heads had appeared around the edges of shacks from the thud of the rock and the tone of the voice, and George knew there was no way of avoiding a fight. It hadn't taken long for word of an impending fight to spread either. It seemed to George that half of the people in Papertown had gathered in the area around them.

Without taking his eyes from Junior, he maneuvered himself so that he wouldn't trip over anything when it started. He also tried to remember all that his Uncle Ward and his dad had taught him about fighting... He didn't have long to wait for Junior to make his move. Semms came at him, and all of George's focus was on the fight from then on.

Junior charged in swinging rock-hard fists with both arms. George ducked in under his wild charge, with knees slightly bent. As Junior's right arm sailed over his head, George grabbed it with both hands and pivoted on his left foot. Junior's weight folded over him and George straightened his knees while holding Junior's arm, throwing Junior over his hip and back in a rolling hip Jiu-Jitsu maneuver. He released Junior's arm as soon as the weight left his back.

Junior flipped completely over in the air and landed on his back in a pile of scrap iron with a loud clang. George could hear the groan from him as he landed, and then realized that if he'd kept holding Junior's arm during the throw, he could have broken it.

Junior wasn't giving up that easy though, and he came back up to his feet with a mixture of pain and anger on his face.

The crowd was hooting and hollering, "Break his bones, break his bones!"

George didn't know if the words were meant for him or Junior.

"Now you're going to get it, Rickson," Junior said.

Before he could finish, George hit him in the throat as hard as he could with his left fist. His right foot was solidly planted and he felt something pop in Junior's throat.

Junior staggered back with his arms wind-milling, then turned to his left away from George, with his shoulders hunched and his arms up, to protect his face and neck. His elbows were straight out in front of him. He made a rasping squawk when George hit him and a wheezing noise after that.

George kicked him as hard as he could behind the right knee and Semms went down as if he'd been hit with a post. Junior managed to get to his hands and knees while George was deciding whether to kick him again, and where to kick him. Thoughts of how Deeter Jompson had kicked Mr. Corbett flashed through George's mind. He didn't want Junior getting up, but he didn't want to go to prison either.

He needn't have worried. Junior could barely stay on his hands and knees, gasping for breath, his face red and his mouth wide open.

"He's choking!" a man yelled, and ran over to Junior, thumping him on the back. This knocked him flat on his face in the dirt.

The man stepped away and George grabbed Junior by the hair. He lifted Junior's head and said, "If you get up, I'll have to kill you."

Junior shook his head in a side-to-side motion with tears in his eyes.

George dropped his head and stepped back, and then looked around to see if anyone was going to interfere. They were all looking at him until he met their gaze.

A different man said, "Whoo-ee I ain't never see'd nothing like that before."

A woman stepped toward Junior who had rolled over onto his side, still wheezing. George glanced down at him once more and then walked through the little crowd and into the woods behind Papertown.

The fight was over almost as fast as it had started. He thought he might be in trouble with Mr. Schmidt, but his worry was unfounded. Harold Schmidt liked George before the fight and, despite his rough talk and cursing; he was a kind man who disliked bullies. Now, he liked George even more.

George's dad woke him quietly in the middle of the night and motioned him outside, holding his finger upright under his nose for quiet. George followed him out, realizing that his mother was still sleeping. When they got about halfway to the privy, his dad stopped him by grabbing his arm just above the elbow. The grasp was firm but not tight, so George knew he wasn't in real bad trouble. His dad had dealt with tough men during his years with the railroad and wasn't one to trifle with.

"Son, I heard about the fight and I'm proud of you. Your mother won't be because she don't hold with fighting. Like I say, I'm proud of you, but I'm worried about you too. You're getting a reputation as a rough customer, someone to be afraid of. That's a reputation not one man in a thousand should have. No matter how well you handled yourself today, you're not a man yet. You don't want a hard man calling you out. Take my word on that."

George nodded his head in the moonlight and said nothing.

His dad placed a hand on his shoulder and said, "Stay low, Son. Stay out of trouble and let others slay the dragons. Life will bring on more than enough before you know it without you charging into it. The man in front is the first target."

George would remember that later——and more than once.

CHAPTER 17

After the fight with Junior Semms, George stayed away from Papertown for a few days.

One Saturday morning, while he was sitting at the kitchen table reading, his mother said, "I believe you have a visitor, George."

He stepped to the door and saw Carrie walking up the driveway. He met her on the back porch and touched her arm, turning her back toward the street with him. They walked a little way before he spoke.

"Hi Carrie, I'm glad to see you," he said.

She glanced at him and replied, "I was beginning to wonder. Don't you want me to meet your mother?"

"It's not that. She would have kept you in there half a day talking your leg off and asking questions, and I don't know how much of that you'd be able to take."

"I can take a lot. And what about my leg? I've got two in case you haven't noticed."

George flushed red. He immediately thought about the scratches on her bare legs the last time he saw her. He remembered wanting to lick the drop of blood from her leg. This time she was wearing a light-blue, cotton, sleeveless dress that came to about four inches below her knees, with a pair of navy-blue, low-cut tennis shoes.

They walked down the road past Papertown and he asked if she was scared to go back into the woods.

She took his hand and said, "Not with you, George. You're my hero."

He blushed again and she laughed and bumped against him with her bare shoulder, tilting her head against him as she did.

They checked to see that there were no cars or people in sight, and then veered off into the woods. A short distance in, they came to a three-strand, barbed-wire fence. He put his foot on the middle wire and lifted up on the top one so she could climb through. She gathered her dress and lifted it to mid-thigh, then tilted her head down in his direction as she stepped between the wires. He could see all of her brassiere and the tops of both breasts as she bent over and the scooped neck of her dress drooped.

"Oh damn," she said.

He pulled his attention from looking down her dress to see that she had one leg through the fence and her dress hem was caught on a barb on the lower strand.

He said, "Hold on." While he held the wire up with one hand, he leaned over the top of her and reached down to free the dress. His fingers brushed her leg and he jerked his hand back.

"Go ahead George, I can't stay like this."

He tried again, this time deliberately brushing his hand down her leg to where the dress was caught. They both giggled as he worked the dress free. George was surprised at her lightheartedness and his own boldness.

She grabbed his hand and held onto it as they went into the woods. "Where are we going, George?"

"Down by the river if you've got time."

"I've got all day. What have you got——a skinny–dipping hole?" she asked as she leaned against him again.

"Maybe," he said as he stopped and turned to face her.

She had her left hand in his right and she reached up behind his neck with her other hand and pulled herself against him. He grabbed her around the waist and pulled against her to keep his balance. The kiss made both of them so dizzy they were staggering in place to keep from falling.

"You just want a big time, don't you?" she asked as she pulled back and smiled up at him.

He didn't know what to say but felt that "no" was the wrong answer, so he didn't speak.

"That's OK. I wouldn't like you if you wasn't a man."

This kind of talk was making George giddy and made it hard for him to walk upright.

She had already noticed and tormented him by brushing against him and saying things like "Look up there, what kind of bird is that?" and, "Have you got something in your pocket, George?"

He was almost to the point of being mad at her but held his tongue. Finally, they reached the river at a point where a wide bend left a still, deep backwater with a firm gravel bottom. Overhead, the sky was clear and pale blue. Thick, blue grass covered the rounded peninsula on a gentle slope to the river. The river forced its way against the rocky bank on the other side, while on their side it was mostly still but alive. Small eddies swirled slowly and died, reappearing at other spots to do the same.

Screwing up his courage, George said, "We could leave our clothes in that tree while we swim." He pointed to a large willow with branches hanging nearly to the ground. The lone tree stood twenty-five yards from the river and the noontime sun painted a large shadowy circle under its branches. Bare spots in the grass showed a tan, sandy soil.

"Oh wow! You do have a skinny-dipping hole. Do you have some-thing else, too?"

"Something else?" he asked dumbfounded, as he watched her pull her dress up over her head.

During the seconds the dress was covering her face he stared at her crotch and could see the powder-puff shadow and blond hair curling out from the sides of her panties. The lump in his throat was nearly as big as the one in his pants. She twisted halfway around and tossed the dress toward the tree.

"A rubber, George?" brought him out of his stupor.

"What?"

"Do you have a rubber?"

"No, I don't," he said with a sinking feeling.

She was standing in front of him in her nearly transparent pink pant-ies and the white brassiere. He couldn't believe things had reached this point. He thought she was too nice a girl to do things like this, a girl who would be a virgin when she was married, and only to a rich, important type. Now, here she was in the open, in her underwear, asking him if he had a rubber.

With a grin, she pulled an unpackaged one out of the top of her brassiere.

"I knew you wouldn't be carrying one and wouldn't have a chance to get one. I stole this from my uncle's dresser drawer. He'll never miss it. Now take off your clothes unless you want me to put mine back on."

George didn't waste any more time and stripped to the waist. She watched as he tried to pull his pants over his shoes and fell over onto his side. She burst out laughing while he lay there untying his shoes, he looked up to see her reach around and unsnap the brassiere from behind. She shrugged her shoulders and it came away from her and straight down her arms. She tossed it onto a branch of the tree, still giggling.

He kicked off his shoes and finally got one leg out of his pants, then stood up as he pulled the other one free without taking his eyes off of her. They were facing each other so close they might bump heads, both of them wearing only underpants.

She hooked her thumbs into her waistband and said, "Ready?" while she stripped them off and stepped out of them, then flung them up onto another limb.

George nearly ruptured himself trying to catch up with her. He could see the sun sparkling in the soft blonde hair between her legs. She turned and ran for the water, and he thought she was the most beautiful thing he'd ever seen. He couldn't bring himself to think of her in terms of a sex object. She was too nice for that.

"Wait," he hollered.

She ran into the water to her waist and then turned back toward him as he stepped out of his own shorts, leaving them where they fell.

"Don't worry; we won't let it go away," she said.

He staggered after her thinking how perfect her breasts were. They pointed straight at him with no lines and no veins, and her complexion was peaches-and-cream perfection topped with large pink nipples. He needed the cold water to keep himself under control.

She met him in waist deep water and they hugged, groped, and kissed each other. He tried to duck down to kiss her breasts and she pushed his head under water. He pulled her under too.

After playing around in the water, they finally stood still in a long passionate kiss. Her tongue entered his mouth then something else entered besides her tongue, startling him.

"Don't lose it and don't bite it," she said, pulling back from him with a big smile.

It was the rubber he'd forgotten all about. He hadn't used one before but wasn't going to worry about it now. Now it was time to get out of the river and under the willow.

It was a time of wonderment for George. His thoughts filled him with images of love and marriage, of living with Carrie in a little white house with a picket fence around it. He hadn't seen a place like that, but had read about it many times.

They lay in the sand completely naked, with his shirt under her head and back to keep sand out of her hair. She lay beside him on her back with her knees drawn up and a dreamy look on her face, while he lay on his side admiring her. He wondered if she was thinking similar thoughts but was afraid to ask. He didn't want to spoil the moment.

They rested until they were dry all over and then cleaned up at the edge of the river, careful to keep their hair dry. She said, "You'll have to get the rubbers next time, George. We could have used two this time. I almost made you eat me." She laughed at the expression on his face. "Don't worry we'll do it next time. I'll do you too."

Even though he wasn't sure what she was talking about, he was surprised to hear her say something like that. Still, at the same time, he wanted to go right back to the willow and do it all again. He couldn't talk the rest of the way back.

CHAPTER 18

George was in Papertown working on a plow for Harold Schmidt a few weeks after the trip to the river with Carrie. He was removing the plowshares so they could be taken to a welding shop to have the points built up with weld. While the plowshares were off, George would clean the rust from the moldboards with a wire brush and sandpaper and then coat them with grease.

As he was doing this, Pootie Barnett, one of the Papertown girls, came up to George and asked how he was doing.

"OK," said George, wondering what she was after.

They weren't unfriendly, but they weren't friends either. She was about four years younger than George and was just showing hard bumps on her chest. She was a cute girl with short brown hair and wide-spaced blue eyes and a pug nose. Her mother had been a friend of Molly Jompson.

He wasn't sure what she knew about him and his encounters with the women in Papertown, but the way she was digging her bare toes into the dirt he figured she was after something.

"What is it, Pootie?"

She surprised him when she said, "I know about you and Molly. Everybody knows about it."

He just grunted and turned back toward the plow.

"You're Okay George and I thought you should know something."

He looked up at her from his kneeling position and saw fear in her eyes. "What is it?" he asked.

"Deeter broke out of prison and he's been around here asking about you and Molly and where she went. He's crazy as a snake so you'd better stay hid for a while."

Before he could say anything, or thank her, she ran off through the weeds with an awkward gait.

He wasn't too concerned about what she said. Molly had left with someone else, and he didn't think anyone had seen the two of them when they were together in the brush. Of course, Molly had probably run off at the mouth about it. He didn't know how Deeter would have found out about it otherwise, and he didn't really care. Somebody would be calling the law on him anyway and he wouldn't dare hang around or cause any trouble.

The next morning George was heading back through Papertown carrying the two plowshares in a burlap bag. Mr. Schmidt had brought them back from the welding shop the previous evening and left them for him. The plow had 16-inch moldboards and the shares were heavy enough that he had the bag slung over his shoulder and was holding the neck with both hands. As he came around the corner of the last shack, a shadow separated from the back of the shack and George's face exploded in a red haze.

He found himself on his back on the plowshares with his face numb and eyes watering so badly he couldn't see. Just as he became aware of where he was, a sudden pounding on the sides of his face brought a surge of panic, fear and numbness. He tried to roll away, but realized he was pinned by a man on top of him. Through the roaring in his ears, he could hear someone with a high-pitched voice shrieking in the background and right above him, the voice of Deeter Jompson.

"Teach you to mess with my woman you little whelp bastard."

Deeter was slapping him alternately left hand, right hand, left hand, making his head roll from side to side while his arms were pinned to his sides by Deeter's knees. He tried to hit Deeter in the back with his knee but it had no effect. All he could see was a black outline and a red background. He tried to think of something he'd been taught that would get him loose, but nothing came to mind. He remembered the savage beating Deeter had given Mr. Corbett and wondered if he would wind up the same way. He finally managed to kick Deeter in the back of the head with the inside of his foot, knocking Deeter's head toward his.

He tried head-butting Deeter's face at the same time and felt a sharp pain at his forehead. Deeter only became more enraged, turning the slaps to punches. George was getting dizzy and starting to really feel the pain. Then he heard another voice, followed by a gunshot.

It sunk in that a man's voice was saying, "The next one's right through your damned head."

Deeter stopped pounding him and George heard a thud and felt a vibration from the impact. Deeter rolled off him with a moan. George rolled the opposite way and scrambled away on all fours with his ears still ringing. As his vision cleared, he saw Pootie's dad, Clovis, pointing an old, lever action, Winchester rifle at Deeter.

He was saying, "Move your worthless ass outta here afore I finish the job."

George never would have believed that the Barnetts would befriend him. Deeter staggered to his feet with his eyes wide and rolling and George realized that Clovis must have hit him on the side of the head with the rifle butt. Deeter, back on his feet, was blinking right down the barrel of the .30-30 from six feet away. For a moment, George thought Deeter was going to charge the smaller Clovis. He looked at Clovis, who had his finger on the trigger and the hammer back. Both George and Deeter knew that Clovis would shoot him if he did. Without a word, Deeter turned and ran toward the woods.

Clovis spit on the ground as he lowered the hammer, and then the rifle. He spoke with a gap-toothed smile to no one in particular, "Learnt that butt-stroke in the Marines. I used it on Japs on the islands but I never thought I'd ever use it on a white man."

Clovis was a medium-sized man with dark hair. He was also a World War II veteran and had fought the Japanese on the island of Okinawa. It occurred to George that he and Clovis were about the same size. George felt hands on him and realized that Pootie's mother and a couple of other women were telling him to lie down so they could "tend to" him.

He lay back with a groan. The wearing off of the adrenaline rush brought the pain on in waves. He couldn't stop himself from moaning and thrashing his legs to try to alleviate the pain, though every motion of his body brought on more pain. His head was pounding and he thought he might throw up.

George's dad and the Sheriff had reached Papertown at the same time. His dad loaded him into their car for the trip to the hospital while the Sheriff got on his radio and called for manpower. Then he took statements from the bystanders. George was too busy moaning and holding wet cloths over his face to know what all was going on. An hour later, after tests, questioning and paperwork, he was in a hospital bed fifteen miles away.

George was found to have two cracked ribs from the plowshares under his back, a broken nose, and a grotesquely swollen head with two black eyes. One eye was swollen completely shut and the other nearly shut. He also had a deep, curved, two-inch-long gash at his hairline from Deeter's upper teeth. Other than the cracked ribs and the nose, there were no broken bones. His nose was splinted from the inside and he had to breathe through a sore mouth with loose teeth. They kept him overnight, but didn't give him any painkillers for fear he might have a concussion.

His mother stayed in the room with him that night, sitting upright in a chair. George couldn't recall ever spending that much quiet time alone with her before. Things had settled down for the evening and the nurses had stopped coming around, when his mother started talking about Linden.

She hadn't really talked to George about Linden since he died and he really didn't want to hear it now. He lay there breathing through his mouth. Just when he thought she was about to burst into tears over Linden, she switched to his being attacked by Deeter Jompson. He looked sideways at her with his one available eye, to see she that had her handkerchief in her hands and was unconsciously wringing it first one way and then the other, as if it were soaked with water.

She said, "I knew about you and Molly Jompson and should have said something. I was worried about you catching something from her and wanted to warn you. I just couldn't accept that my son was doing that. You've grown up so fast that at times I can look right at you and not recognize you." Then she did start crying and couldn't talk for a few minutes.

George had difficulty talking too, and could only croak, "It's OK, Mom."

When she gathered herself together, she said, "I should have warned you about that. You know. Woman stuff, and about jealous husbands too. It's a mother's duty to prepare her boy for the ways of life."

George rasped, "Well I know now and I ain't wanted nothing to do with Molly Jompson for a long time anyway. I'll be OK."

The rest of the night was a silent bond between them and both slept intermittently. He would wake up occasionally with random pains, to see her dozing, still upright, but with her chin dropped straight down onto her chest. He didn't know what kept her from falling over. It was the closest George remembered being to his mother.

His nose and torso were both re-taped and he had a painful ride home the next day. Afterwards, George found out that Deeter had been hunted down with dogs and treed like a coon just before midnight. He had outrun and outsmarted the dogs for over twelve hours. It was said he was so exhausted and torn up from briars, that they had to carry him out in chains and weren't too careful how they did it. Word was that Deeter Jompson would be in the state penitentiary for a good many more years.

George learned that anyone could be overcome by another person under certain circumstances. He resolved to never again walk blindly around, over or under anything. The helpless feeling he'd had with Deeter on top of him was burned-in. He had plenty of time to think about what he might have done differently and what would have happened to him if other people hadn't intervened.

He silently promised himself that he would never again take a beating from another man without giving as much as he got. He knew that he needed more than what he'd been taught though. The comment from Clovis Barnett about the butt-stroke stuck in his mind. He made himself a vow to learn more about using weapons and to always be aware of what might be available for use.

On the way home from the hospital they stopped at a drug store so his mother could buy gauze and liniment.

While she was out of the car, his dad told him, "I warned you this might happen. If Clovis had already left for the day you'd probably have been killed or crippled. I don't know what all you've been getting into and don't want you to tell me because I don't want to lie to your Mother. I'll have to tell her what I guess as it is, but guessing isn't lying.

"What I'm telling you is this. As soon as you finish high school, and have turned eighteen, you are on your own, Son.

"You've been in more serious trouble than a grown man normally would, and you're going to bring too much grief home to roost. Start working and saving your money now. You're going to need it. When you leave home, maybe your Papertown friends will take you in if you want to live like that. There will be no more trouble involving this family. That's all I have to say about it for now."

The warning had been too late, but George kept his mouth shut. He was surprised that his mother seemed to know more about what he'd been doing than his father did. He sure didn't want to live like the Papertown people either. He didn't even want to see them living like that, even though some of them were worthless in his opinion. He speculated that he'd felt that way about Clovis Barnett too, without really knowing him. He thought that maybe someone isn't bad unless you really see that person doing something bad to someone else. He knew for sure that Deeter Jompson was bad because he had seen it a number of times and had experienced it firsthand.

CHAPTER 19

George speculated on what his dad would have done if attacked by Deeter Jompson as he had been. He just couldn't imagine his dad being caught unawares though, especially after being warned. George felt like a fool. He knew for sure that if Deeter had attacked his dad, the outcome would have been totally different. George had seen his dad engage in violence twice.

The first time had been at a railroad picnic during better times. In that encounter, his dad interrupted a half-drunk bully who was pushing a smaller man around. The bully had pushed or tossed the smaller man up onto a picnic table. He held the man down with one meaty hand at his throat while alternately tickling him like a child and poking him in the stomach and ribs with stiffened fingers of the other hand.

The man on his back was huffing and wheezing, gasping for breath, begging him to stop, his face a bright, reddish purple as he alternately writhed sideways and tried to roll away. The bully kept repeating, "Pumpkin eater, pumpkin eater."

Pete Rickson was passing by and casually suggested, "why don't you pick on someone more your own size, Kuwalsky, like a fat old woman." It was apparent that George's dad and the bully knew each other and had a mutual dislike.

The bully, his dad's height but forty pounds heavier, enraged and too boozed up to know better, turned away from his victim and shouted, "You!" He swung a wild haymaker at Pete's head.

Pete casually moved his beer bottle from his right hand to his left and shifted his weight to his left. The bully's fist sailed over his right shoulder. In the same movement, George's dad countered by sinking his right fist into the bully's soft spot just below the breastbone.

The man folded like an accordion from the right hook and fell face down, retching. Pete Rickson kicked him hard in the rump one time, and then walked away with a smile on his face. He had neither raised his voice nor spilled his beer. There hadn't been time for the typical cry of "Fight!" but enough people saw it happen, that word spread rapidly.

They heard later that the Bully had to crawl away and limped for a month. No one seemed disappointed in the outcome and the bully wasn't talking about it.

The second time George saw the violence from his dad, there was much more rage in it, but it was controlled rage. This was an incident involving school and George himself.

Throughout his school years, George maintained good grades and hadn't had any trouble with classes or teachers.

A year before though, when George was fourteen, one teacher became an exception. The ninth-grade math teacher, Mr. Frank Yount, liked to pick on the boys and pat the girls on their butts. Yount was a solidly built man in his early forties. He was bald on top, with thick gray hair on the back and sides of his head. He had a rugged look and piercing blue eyes, even when wearing his reading glasses. George noticed he especially liked picking on Papertown kids. He would do any number of things to humiliate boys who displeased him. Punishments ranged from sucking on a baby-bottle nipple in class, to dropping their pants in front of the class to receive a whipping from his ventilated paddle. Dropping the pants was most embarrassing to those who might have dirty, stained or ragged underwear.

One boy resisted dropping his pants, saying, "I ain't got no drawers on." Yount grabbed the kid and swung him around, slamming him into the wall. Then Yount upended a nearly full trashcan over the boy's head. He forced the trashcan clear to the kid's shoulders, knocking him to his knees. Next, Yount made the boy clean up the mess on his hands and knees and lick the floor before leaving. The students were all so humbled; most of them never told their parents.

One day George got in trouble and the cause was two boys from town, one on either side, shooting spit-wads at each other. George had reared back in his seat to avoid being hit in the face and his movement caught the teacher's eye.

Yount ordered George, and Walter Olson, the one who shot the last spit-wad, to the back of the room. He had both of them stand at attention against the wall while he marched down the center aisle toward them. As all eyes watched, he grabbed the smaller boy by the shirtfront and hoisted him up the wall. He was able to reach high enough that the boy's loose shirttail caught on a coat hook. This left the boy with his shirt bunched up under his arms and his feet dangling.

Yount grabbed George next. George had seen him do this before and wasn't going to be a willing participant. He was almost as tall as Yount, but fifty pounds lighter. When Yount grabbed his shirt and attempted to lift, George's knee came up first and caught the teacher in the groin. As Yount bent forward, George braced himself against the wall and was able to push the staggering teacher away from him with both hands.

Knowing there was no resolution, George ran from the room and left for home before Yount could recover enough to grab him. George began the long walk home, not waiting the two hours for the bus. After more than two-and-a-half hours of walking, he saw the bus crossing the road ahead of him. It stopped and waited for him.

Bus driver, Melvin Barnes, said, "Come on George. You can ride the rest of the way. You ain't hurt my feelings none."

That evening when his dad came home, George was waiting. Somehow, his dad already knew he had been in trouble.

"Tell me why you've been expelled, George?" he said.

George told exactly what happened without mentioning the things that Yount had done to others in the past.

His dad looked at him and said, "There's more than this. Now tell me."

George did. His dad left in his car shortly thereafter and was gone for more than three hours. He said nothing when he came home.

The next morning George's mother woke him at the regular time and said, "Get ready for school. Your father will drive you."

George didn't question how he would be able to get back in school. It was a fifteen-mile ride to the school at the county seat. George and his dad were both silent for the first few miles.

Finally, his dad said, "Did you ever hear of Yount doing anything more to those boys or girls than what you've already told me?" Before George could respond his dad said, "Like making them suck on him?"

George was surprised, because his dad had never talked to him about anything like that before. He just said, "No."

George knew that he must have talked to some of the other parents, because he hadn't heard of anything like that himself.

"Don't ever let a man do anything like that to you," his dad said.

"Not likely," said George.

His dad just nodded, without looking at George, as if to affirm something in his own mind. Finally, he said, "Don't ever repeat any of this conversation."

This time he did look at George, who said, "I won't."

They were silent for the remainder of the trip. When they got there, his dad said, "Take me directly to the Principal's office."

When they got out of the car, George noticed three other men getting out of their cars too. He assumed they were also parents. They all assembled in the principal's office, with George being the only student.

Mr. Andrews, the principal, was a small, slightly built man with wavy brown hair and a pencil-thin moustache, who always wore a gray flannel suit.

Pete Rickson addressed him, "Mr. Andrews, Yount has been assaulting and humiliating lots of kids. George is in here with me because he's a witness, and he's not a liar."

The principal started to protest in his squeaky voice, "You can't come in here accusing one of our teaching staff like that."

"The hell I can't," George's dad said. "He belongs in prison and you should be there with him for condoning his actions. Now get that son of a bitch in here and I'll accuse him to his face."

George had never heard his dad use those words or swear so vehemently.

At the word prison, the principal turned pale and stammered, "OK, OK, we can work this out."

At that moment, Frank Yount appeared on his own, apparently believing he could power over parents as well as students.

George's dad said, "My son tells me you put your hands on him and you've been abusing the other kids as well. Is that true, George?"

"Yes sir," George said.

Yount said, "He caught me by surprise and kicked me in the groin. I wasn't going to hang him on a hook like I did the Olson kid. He can't kick no teacher in this state."

At these words, the principal looked like he was going to throw up. One of the other three men rose halfway out of his chair in anger. George guessed that it was Walter Olson's father.

George's dad said, "You hung the Olson boy and you would have hung George if he had let you. He can damned sure defend himself in this state or any other. You slimy prick. You can't even handle kids, let alone the law. Why don't you try some of your sick shit on me and see what happens?"

Pete Rickson was getting madder by the minute. He was slightly taller than Yount, but was still lighter by twenty or thirty pounds. They were about the same age. George had no doubt his dad was about to explode and he saw that Yount's face was purple with white blotches.

Frank Yount wasn't as good a judge of men as he was of boys. He grabbed Pete Rickson's shirtfront with his left hand while drawing back his right fist.

George realized that this was what his dad was waiting for and he saw a momentary glint in his father's eye as he went into action. With his right hand, he grabbed Yount's left thumb and bent it downward so fast and so hard, George heard the bone snap. At the same time, with his other arm, he blocked Yount's right hand punch and slammed the heel of his left hand into the end of his nose.

Yount bellowed and spun away. He flopped over sideways and then onto the floor, slinging blood all over the office on his way down. George and the three men jumped from their chairs, overturning them, and scrambled to get out of the way. The principal crawled under his desk and tried to pull the desk phone down with him. Mr. Olson reached over and yanked the cord out of the wall socket.

George thought the fight was over but his dad wasn't finished yet. Yount was trying to crawl past the overturned chairs and out the door on his hands and knees, favoring his left arm.

Pete Rickson yelled, "Here's one from me, you bastard!" He caught Yount from behind with a solid kick to the crotch.

Yount curled up in a ball moaning, gasping, and blowing blood with his breath like something live was caught in his throat. The seat of his pants grew wet. George's dad grabbed him by the shirt collar with one hand and the belt at his back with the other. Then he half-lifted, half-carried him down the hall, leaving a trail of blood and urine. Two of the other men ran ahead of them and held the double doors open at the front of the school.

Pete Rickson threw Yount down at the top of the steps and watched him tumble to the bottom. "Don't come back unless you're ready for prison," he said with a growl.

George followed the procession and was surprised to see that there were students standing all along the halls cheering, and a number of adults present in the schoolyard. Two of the women teachers went to Yount's aid and shortly thereafter, helped him get into his car. George and Pete Rickson watched them and then went to their own car.

On the way home neither George nor his dad said a word until they were nearly home. At that point, his dad said,

"If you ever hit a man in the nose like that be careful how you do it. If you strike upward at too much of an angle, you can drive his nose up into his brain and kill him. That stuff's for wars."

George understood but only nodded. When they got home, he went to the backyard and sat on the back-porch steps while his dad went inside. George heard him tell his mom what happened.

"I lost control today, Mother. It went way beyond what I intended. They're likely to send the deputies out to get me. Call Hardy if they do."

George knew that Hardy was a lawyer sometimes used by the railroad. He didn't hear his mother's response.

The Sheriff came out that evening, but didn't take Pete Rickson away. The two of them sat in the patrol car in the driveway for an hour. Occasionally George would see puffs of smoke come out of the windows from the Sheriff's cigar. Twice, he saw the Sheriff raise his microphone to his face. Finally, George saw his dad reach across and shake hands with the Sheriff.

He got out of the car and the Sheriff left. George went back to school the next day, taking the forty-five-minute ride on the school bus as he normally would. A substitute teacher took over the math class for the rest of the term. Later George heard from a classmate that several other parents wanted to press criminal charges against Frank Yount, but he was allowed to leave the county instead.

Parents of several girls wanted Yount behind bars for life. Parents of a few boys wanted his mouth shut permanently.

One of the older boys said, "Your old man's OK, George. Everybody's glad he whipped Yount's ass."

George heard later from other kids that Yount had been having sex with both boys and girls in a storage closet next to his classroom. There was wild speculation about what they had been doing and who the participants were.

CHAPTER 20

arrie came around to see George twice during the first two weeks he was home from the hospital. The first time he was still so stiff and sore he couldn't go beyond his back porch. Consequently, it was the first time Carrie met his mother.

Later, George's mom told him she liked Carrie, but said, "That girl is putting on airs." George wasn't sure what she meant by that, but didn't say anything.

George and Carrie stayed on the porch while his mom went back inside. With his mother just inside the house, it wasn't much of a personal visit. They had to strain for conversation with Carrie doing most of the talking.

Carrie was wearing pastel-green pedal-pushers, white sandals and a sleeveless button-down blouse. George's heart ached just to touch her. The thought of her lying on her back naked with her head on his belly made it difficult for him to breathe, especially with the sharp pains from the cracked and taped ribs.

She told George that the people in Papertown were bad, crazy trash and that she wouldn't' have anything to do with them herself.

George said nothing.

By the second visit, he was feeling better and they walked down the road a ways. This time she was wearing pink, just-above-the-knee shorts and boy's black, *Red Ball Jets* tennis shoes, without socks. The top was a sleeveless, collarless pullover that emphasized her ample breasts.

She said she could tell he was still sore and thought his face sure looked funny now that the tape and splints were removed from his nose.

The eye swelling was gone but both eyes were ringed with a rainbow of color, with purple and dark yellow being predominate.

She giggled and said, "You look like a bandit."

The bandit was able to kiss and feel some, but she held him back from more than that.

"I don't want to hurt you, George. There'll be time for that later."

A thought flashed through his mind that he didn't know if she meant hurt him later, or have sex later. Thinking about the sex, he let it go at that. He was ready to try anything she would let him do. Her last words from the trip to the river were still ringing in his ears. After this second visit, he didn't see her again for a long time. The words she had just spoken would come back to haunt him later.

CHAPTER 21

George was cutting weeds around the farm equipment with a weed whip one morning when a redheaded boy about nine years old came running his way from the woods. He was heading straight toward the shacks and didn't seem to be aware of George. The kid was gasping from either fear or lack of breath from the exertion. George could see tear streaks coursing down his dirty face as he ran past.

"Hey what's the matter?" George hollered at him. George didn't know all of the younger kids anymore and didn't know this one, though he had noticed him before.

"They're killing my dog!" the boy sobbed as he fell from trying to stop too fast.

"Where are they?" George asked. He remembered seeing the boy leading a half-grown mongrel around with a piece of binder-twine knotted around its neck. He also knew that all the men who were sober had already left for the day.

"You gotta save him!" the boy cried as he staggered to his feet. He made a grab for George's weed whip.

George said, "I'll hang onto this. Just tell me who and show me where,"

"It's Billy Allen and his bunch, and there's four of them," the kid said as he stopped to catch his breath.

George was already heading back the way the kid came from and motioned him to lead. George knew Billy Allen as another troublemaker who avoided trouble with him. He was a year or two younger than George, but about the same size. George didn't doubt he could handle him, but didn't know who the others were though. In the back of his mind was the warning the doctor had given him. "Don't get hit on the nose again this year." There was a long time yet to go.

He needn't have worried. When George entered the clearing with the other boy looking on, he raised his weed whip in an attempt cut the twine tying the dog to the small, scrub tree. He yelled "Run!" at the same time to stop what was going on. The upraised whip and the yell made the whole bunch scatter like chickens. They had been throwing jackknives at the tied dog from behind a line scratched into the leaves and dirt.

A small, homemade shank knife was hanging from the wounded animal's hip and a larger jackknife lay on the ground near it. The animal was hunkered down and whimpering at the end of the rope farthest from the people tormenting it. The boy, whose name George finally remembered as Ernest Wales, was whimpering with almost the same sound as the dog. When George approached the frightened animal, it snapped at him and nearly bit him.

Ernest also approached, and was bitten. George threw down the weed whip, took off his shirt, and with his arms through both sides, folded the shirt down and around the dog's head, blindfolding it. Ernest was finally able to soothe it while George pulled the shank out of its hip and cut the twine loose from the tree with it. The boys had been at it for a while and the dog was bleeding from several puncture wounds.

Still crying and talking to the dog, Ernest removed the blindfold. The animal shivered and then relaxed in his arms, as if it knew salvation was at hand.

They wrapped its torso in George's shirt and started back toward Papertown. As tired as he was, the boy wouldn't give up his dog for George to carry. They took the dog to the Wales' shack, Ernest hollering, "Ma, Ma," when they got close.

His large, red-haired and sunburned mother, Esther, came out to see what the disturbance was. Esther had a mop of frizzy red hair that fell well below her shoulders and the complexion of a true redhead. George noticed she even had freckles on her full lips.

At first, she thought George was the guilty party, but after Ernest explained she said, "Them little whelps. When your old man gets home, we're going down to the Allens' and beat some ass."

From the fire in her eyes, George believed that the 'old man' wouldn't be needed. His immediate concern was to explain a blood-soaked shirt to his own mother. Toward the other end of the row of shacks, he could see someone with Billy Allen near his shack. Still carrying his weed whip and with the bloodied shirt tossed over his shoulder, he headed that way.

Billy Allen, another towhead, was big for his age but had a small up-tilted nose, giving him a Porky-Pig look. He was sitting on a railroad tie step, digging at his fingernails with a homemade skinning knife that looked like it was made from a bastard file. Two of Billy's friends were standing nearby but George didn't know them. He looked each of them in turn straight in the eye. Neither was as big as he or Billy.

"Hey George," Billy said. Billy was the first to break eye contact.

"Anybody lose a knife?" George asked. Three heads all shook no in unison. George pulled the jackknife from his pants pocket and pointed to the shank in his belt. "Cut yourself Billy?" he asked.

Billy glanced at the dried blood on his knife and momentarily got even dumber looking. "Uh, I cleaned some squirrel with it," he answered.

George laughed and said, "I reckon you'll be having the Waleses over for dinner then." He took a swipe with the weed whip at a patch of weeds within a few inches of Billy's feet and said, "See you later, Billy."

Billy fell over backwards against the shack, yanking his feet up, and the other two jumped back nearly three feet. George left them like that. He knew that the Waleses would settle-up, at least with the Allens. People didn't call in the law for something like this.

George found out later that Mrs. Wales had punched Billy's dad in the mouth and knocked him down. He didn't fight back, saying, with a bloody split lip, "You're just taking advantage cause you know I cain't hit no woman."

People nearby laughed because they knew he'd hit his own woman and his kids plenty of times. It would have been over except that the Wales' dog died two days later. The following night, after midnight, a live skunk was dropped through an open window into the Allen shack. The whole family was sprayed and the resulting commotion woke up everyone in the area. The Allens had been shamed twice and no one doubted that the feud would continue. It seemed like there was always one going on in Papertown.

CHAPTER 22

One evening, when George was nearly healed, Harold Schmidt came calling on the Ricksons. After pleasantries and a cup of coffee, he got down to business. "Pete, I've got an opportunity for both of us to make some money on. George too. The County Co-Op wants to build a new, modern elevator up in Dent. The opportunity is in tearing down and removing the old one. They will pay a good price for that, and we get to keep the lumber too. I can get the job, but I can't do it alone. I would like to cut you and George in on it. I need partners I can trust."

"That sounds like a big job, Harold. That old elevator must be eighty feet tall. Are you sure we could do it?"

"One hundred feet tall, and I've got a bulldozer and cables lined up for the job once I'm sure I'll get the help."

"Bulldozer?"

"Yep, we'll pull her over. I've got more than one idea on how to do that."

"Let me think it over, Harold. You know I could only work on weekends."

"A weekend would be all it would take to get her down. George could work on dismantling it on weekdays until school starts up again. You and I could load and haul off the sections on weekends. They'll allow two months to get the area clear, but it has to be finished by Labor Day."

"OK, I'll let you know tomorrow," Pete said.

That night, Pete and Lois discussed it behind closed doors, so George never heard the actual details. The next evening, Pete went over to the Schmidts' while George was working on farm equipment. George saw his dad and Harold shaking hands and knew from the handshake that it was a done deal. He was tired of working on plowshares and cultivator shoes and was excited at the prospect of something new.

The next Friday evening, the three of them drove over to see the elevator in Pete's car and stopped to look at the bulldozer along the way. During the trip, Pete and Harold explained about the construction of elevators and how they worked.

The bulldozer was a 1947 Caterpillar D8. George had driven the old Diamond T truck, even though he didn't have a driver's license, and he hoped to learn how to drive the bulldozer, too.

The town of Dent consisted of a center circle of about one hundred yards inside diameter surrounded by a sidewalk and then a paved street. On each side, county roads branched off at a tangent, not aligning in their north-south or east-west directions. A general store with a gas station, a church and a tavern clustered to the north, and on opposite sides of their respective intersections.

The two gas pumps, dispensing regular and ethyl, sat in front of the store only a car width off the street, and were too close to the building to access on that side. Traffic coming from the wrong side would have turn around and come back. They were still the old-fashioned kind, where you had to pump the gas up into a glass reservoir to the desired amount, up to five gallons at a time, with a hand crank.

The inside of the circle had been parceled out into lots and houses, some of which had already been razed. On the railroad side, to the southern half of the circle, sat smaller houses originally occupied by railroad and elevator laborers, and a couple of dilapidated two-story houses. The northern side, quieter, and not as dusty when trains or trucks rolled past, contained the larger houses and yards of higher-paid yard bosses and office managers.

The ground sloped slightly uphill from the railroad and a two-foot high concrete curb, tapering off to the north, kept the ground inside the circle on a level. Halfway around, where the concrete reached a normal curb height, a wrought iron, spear-tipped, spiked-rail fence continued on, guarding the property of those more fortunate.

Seventy-five yards south of the roundabout street, the railroad ran due east and west. The elevator and its loading, unloading and parking areas stood just north of the tracks creating a fifty-yard open area between the elevator and the street. No houses or businesses resided along the road heading south of the railroad.

They drove around the circle and surveyed the elevator and the area surrounding it. The next day, they went back to start work. George got to drive the truck, while Pete and Harold rode in Harold's car.

The old, all-wooden grain elevators were a serious fire and explosion hazard from the highly flammable grain dust and chaff. Some of the fires and explosions were triggered by lightning strikes, others by careless workers striking a spark with tools, or smoking. George had heard of multiple elevator deaths from a single fire and explosion.

This old elevator stood 60 feet tall to the bottom of the first roofline. A pitched roof skirted the upper section and another covered the top. The top section stood centered over the lower portion.

The elevator base was rectangular at about 40 feet by 60 feet. The upper 40 feet was a smaller rectangle, approximately 30 feet by 40 feet. An annexed office area sat on one side at ground level. Grain bins in the lower

60 feet were built from rough-sized two-by-six lumber laid flat. Bins in the upper 40 feet were constructed from two-by-fours laid flat. George knew that finished lumber was actually smaller than its stated size, but this was all unfinished lumber.

On the inside corners of the bins, angled, horizontal corner braces, about four feet long and of the same lumber, were lapped into the outside corners of the building from bottom to top, and spaced three feet apart. Deep grooves ate into some of the inside lumber from tons of grain sliding against it over the years, and in some places the grooves were worn halfway through the lumber. The rich grain was patterned with alternating dark and light woods, with the lighter part of the wood being softer and worn deeper.

The top floor of the upper structure was called the head-house and was the distribution point for grain filling the bins below it through a ductwork system called a garner. Grain fed up into it through an outside belted-elevator system that began at ground level at the front of the building.

A farmer would drive his truck up onto a scale to be weighed. After that, a motorized chain hoist lifted the front end of the truck several feet into the air to dump the grain into a hopper below. Meanwhile, another hoist opened a steel trap door to accept the dump. Afterwards, the truck was weighed again.

During its progress, and before beginning its trip to the top, the grain went through a filtering process to remove chaff and debris. After that, it would be checked for moisture content. These factors would determine the farmer's final payout.

Manned access to the top section was originally by an outside-mounted, counterweighted dumbwaiter, and then steps with hand-railings across the lower roof pitch to a small door. Structural engineers had deemed the dumbwaiter unsafe to use long before, and it had been previously dismantled and removed. The steps and railings were still in place on the roof, but egress from the head-house led only to a sheer drop to certain death.

Harold was too fat and too heavy to climb the vertical, iron-rung ladders bolted to the inside walls, so Pete and George did the climbing. Each carried a gunnysack tied with a short rope slung over his shoulder. Each sack held 100 feet of clothesline rope, 100 feet of half-inch hemp rope, a Tee-headed wrecking bar, some 20-penny nails, cable clamps, a 12" Crescent wrench and a hammer. The two opposing ladders went up into the top section to just above a window on each side. As he climbed, George counted nine levels above the ground floor and the ladders passed through a hinged trap door at each level.

The windows at every level had a single swing-down shutter on the inside to cover them when grain filled the bins, then a curtain of heavy canvas came down when the shutter was lowered, covering the cracks. There were several bins on every level and some of them were separated by man-sized sliding doors. Others were accessed only through the trap doors above and below. Canvas curtains covered the doors on the inside as well. With the doors closed, the weight of the grain sealed them tight. George speculated that bins on the side the doors were mounted on would have to be filled first to keep the pressure-weight of the grain from tearing them from the tracks.

All of the bins had metal drainpipes with diverter valves that could either let the grain pour down to the bin below, or route it to a central drain chute that was ducted to the outside for filling rail cars. All of the metal piping and ductwork had been removed by others prior to Harold's acquiring the elevator. The outside elevators used to fill the bins through the head-house were also gone when he made the deal.

The view from the top level was higher than George had ever been. He could see the pattern of the town and intersecting roads, surrounded by square and rectangular fields and sections of forest below. At least 3 miles away, he could see glimpses of sunlight glinting on the Kankakee River.

Below him, he saw a few people looking up at the top of the elevator and others standing or walking around in their yards. A single car drove into the town from the west, circled around the residential area, and drove off to the north, getting smaller and smaller until it was out of sight.

George thought that by tying a half-inch rope around his chest for safety, and with Pete feeding it as he went, he would be able to climb out onto the lower roof and drag the end of a clothesline rope, tied to another half-inch, rope around to encircle the top. That wasn't to be. The roof pitch was so steep and the wind so strong, that he couldn't let go of the door-frame. The old stair railing seemed too weak to trust when he ducked under it. Pete tried, with George snubbing the safety rope around a corner brace, but he had no better luck. "We won't make enough money off of this to pay for a funeral. We'll try something else," was his dry comment.

Working from the ladders, they pried the two shutters loose from the opposing window frames and let them fall to the floor. With lumber from them, Pete fashioned a heavy toggle made of spliced, overlapping two-by-sixes. He got some of the longer pieces by prying them up from the floor at the side of the room. He pulled nails free with a wrecking bar, straightened them with a hammer, and reused them, saving the new nails.

While Pete was doing that, George was busy pulling a half-inch rope up from the ground below. He'd tossed one end of his clothesline rope out over the skirted roof, down to Harold.

After tying one end of a half-inch rope to the clothesline, Harold got busy fastening a one-inch rope to the other end. A two-inch rope came next and he fastened the end of that to a one-inch steel cable.

While George was pulling, Pete interrupted his construction project long enough to feed the upper ends of the rope back down through the trap doors on one side.

George reached his limit when he started hoisting two-inch rope and steel cable. Pete pitched in and it took all they had to get the steel cable up through the window. Harold had gotten a workout on the ground, working the knots and joints past the edge of the roof overhang by swinging it back and forth in the wind. The cable couldn't be knotted, so the larger rope and cable were spliced together with cable clamps. The clamps seemed to hang up on everything they passed. They could hear snatches of Harold's cursing from down below when the winds shifted or abated.

The three of them had forgotten to bring a saw, so Pete used the sharp edge of his wrecking bar and his hammer to chop notches around the corners at the center of his makeshift wooden toggle. He and George wrapped the steel cable around that. Both of them stood on the long end of the cable with one foot. Pete pushed the short end down with his other foot while George installed the cable clamps using the Crescent wrenches.

Pete braced himself against George's back to increase his leverage, and they gradually worked the clamps closer and closer to the bundle by leapfrogging them. Both of them were exhausted and had to rest before continuing.

They unclamped the rope from the end of the cable. Then, five feet from the bundle, they made a loop in the cable and passed it around a smaller toggle. They installed a clamp where the cable crossed itself, letting the weight of the cable coming through the window pull itself tight. The smaller toggle would keep the weight of the main toggle from pulling the cable on through the window and down to the ground.

"Wait!" Pete said. That would put all of the strain on the clamp. It won't hold." They had to pull some of the cable back up so that they could work a loop around the main toggle to make a knot around the smaller toggle. Then they finished by adding a clamp on both sides of the knot where it crossed itself.

They quit for the day and untied the different sized ropes from each other on the way down. It had been a long tiring day.

The next morning, a Sunday, they were back up at Dent after breakfast at the Schmidts'.

Pete and George climbed back up to the upper level windows while Harold busied himself on the ground. He checked the D8 bulldozer's oil and water and then unloaded it the from the Lowboy semi-trailer that he'd borrowed. After that, he attached the cable to the drawbar.

Pete's spliced-construction wooden toggle, made from the shutters and pried up floorboards, weighed nearly a hundred pounds. The weight of the cable dragging on it added another twenty or thirty pounds. Working together, He and George hoisted it up onto their shoulders and worked it through the window. The rough lumber drove splinters through their shirts and nearly invisible strands from the steel cable penetrated their heavy leather gloves and stabbed their fingers as they worked. "We're sure as hell earning our money on this one," Pete commented.

Pete, who was worried that his son would get hurt, tripped over the cable and lost his grip. He caught his fall by bracing his hand against the window frame but George couldn't hold the weight by himself and the inside toggle slammed against the window frame. The pinkie and ring fingers of Pete's left hand were smashed between the end of it and the wall. Pete bellowed like a bull.

George couldn't pull it away, so he ran and got one of the wrecking bars. It worked. He was able to pry the end of the toggle up just enough for his dad to pull free. Pete pulled his glove off and poured out blood and two fingernails. "Son of a bitch! That's my fault. If that toggle hadn't held, that cable could have grabbed our ankles and yanked us right out the window!"

George didn't say anything. He hadn't thought of the consequences either. He grabbed Pete's hand and looked at the smashed fingers. They were flattened down to less than a half-inch thick and seemed three times as wide. Then they started to swell. Black blood clotted up where the fingernails had been.

Down on the ground, they could hear the bulldozer. Pete grabbed up the glove and forced it back on, wincing as he did so. "We'd better get back down there before he pulls this damn thing down with us in it." He flexed his fingers. "At least my fingers aren't broken."

"It's a good thing I wasn't wearing my wedding ring, it would have been smashed and the swelling would have cut off my circulation. I learned a long time ago to take it off while I'm working."

They scrambled down the ladders as fast as they dared. George went down first at Pete's insistence. "You're faster," he stated as he motioned for George to go on.

By the time they reached the ground, Harold was taking up the slack in the cable.

George and Pete grabbed the ropes and dragged them away, coiling them as they went. They never took their eyes off the cable while they worked. As it rose from the ground, George glanced around and saw that a number of people were gawking at their actions, more people than could possibly live in this little town.

Pete noticed too, and hollered, "Stay well back everyone. We don't know what's going to happen!"

He continued shouting. "When it does come down, there will be splinters and nails flying through the air like bullets!"

He had to chase away one man who was trying to take up-close photos with a Brownie Hawkeye camera.

Harold couldn't hear anything but the D8 bulldozer. He tightened the cable and the old elevator seemed to shimmer. Harold increased the throttle and the building shivered and groaned. The top seemed to move.

Harold pushed the foot throttle to *wide open*.

The building trembled and swayed.

The bulldozer started digging trenches in the dirt but the building didn't fall.

Harold backed off the throttle, kicked the machine out of gear and waved George over. "The hell, George. I'm going to have to move over and have a run at it. I need you to pull the cable back so I don't run over it when I back up."

George kept the cable out from under the D8 tracks while Harold backed up. He had the D8 lined up at only a slightly different angle, but on fresh ground.

Harold glanced around once more to be sure everyone was clear then kicked the machine back into gear. He mashed the throttle to full-on and worked the levers so the bulldozer ploughed straight ahead.

The cable pulled tight. The tall building swayed and started to topple. With a loud crack, it straightened back up. Simultaneous with the loud crack, was a short, high-pitched whistling and then a tremendous bang that people heard two miles away.

The bottom cable had snapped. The end connected to the bulldozer whipped through the air, just missing Harold's head, and hit the front-mounted dozer blade. It left a one-inch dent in the top flange.

Harold hit the kill switch and jumped down. His ears were ringing from both the cable whistling past his head and his wife's admonishment against working on Sundays. "The Lord will smite you!" she'd said.

"The show is over folks. There won't be anything more today." Pete hollered.

In just a few minutes, the crowd was gone——all except for a girl. She was still standing there, not too far back, looking at George. Pete and George had taken their shirts off and were busily prying splinters from the toggle out of each other's shoulders with Pete's pocketknife. George had barely noticed her before, but now he took a second look. She was petite and cute, with red, wavy hair. She wore a light-colored, flowered dress and stood with her hands clasped in front of her.

Too young, flashed through George's mind.

"Come on George. We've got work to do," Pete said.

George snapped out of it and started loading ropes and tools into the truck bed. Pete and Harold were examining the broken cable. He heard Harold say, "We only need to replace this last cable. All the rest of it is good."

Pete said, "I'm going to see Doc Ingwell. They'll have to cut this glove off of my hand."

George glanced back. The girl was gone.

The next Saturday they were back with Pete's hand wrapped in a bandage as big as a boxing glove. Pete and Harold had a discussion in Pete's car on the way up while George was driving the truck. Harold said, "All we need to do is replace that weak, old cable. I have a brand new one."

"No, we need to do more. I've been thinking about it and I brought tools. There's a crosscut saw and more cable in the back of that truck."

"The hell, you say."

Pete said, "Here's what we need to do. We'll cut through the sidewall at both ends, at ground level, on the side you want it to fall on. Then we'll use the dozer to rip out a section of wall. If that don't cause it to fall, it will at least weaken it enough to pull it over from the top."

"By God, I believe that will work, but how are you going to cut through the walls?"

"Well, we can't cut crossways, we'd hit nail after nail and ruin the saw but I've got two braces and several bits. We'll bore holes one-above-the-other about five feet high to make a vertical slot we can get the crosscut blade through and do the same thing on each end. We'll cut straight down three feet. That should do it. Oh! And we'll bore holes in the middle of the wall at the same heights. We will hook the cable through them and pull the whole section out."

It took the three of them two hours to bore the holes, remove one handle from the saw blade for each cut, work it through, re-bolt it, make the cut, then repeat the process. Pete had previously decided to remount the handles upside down to make the cuts as a draw rather than a push.

They rotated rest breaks, so one rested while the other two worked. Pete could only use one hand, so George and Harold did most of the sawing. The upside-down handles did seem to make the sawing easier.

After a quick lunch break, Harold fired up the D8 and yanked the section of wall. It broke in the middle and left a gaping hole with the ends sticking out at a 30-degree angle. The building shuddered but stayed upright. They debated pulling away at the broken ends from each side but were afraid the building would fall in the wrong direction and land in the street or on the railroad tracks. Pete had previously scheduled with the railroad, to make sure that no trains came through while they were pulling it down.

Finally, Harold hooked his new cable to the one still hanging from the upper level window. He had come back during the week with some metal barn roofing and built a shield around the seat platform on the bulldozer.

This time he went back to his original plan of a slow steady pull. There were several loud cracks. He couldn't see behind him, but he could feel the tension as he pulled. He stomped the throttle to full-bore to stay ahead of the building. It creaked and groaned but it still didn't come over.

George called out for his dad over the roar of the bulldozer.

Pete turned toward him with a questioning look.

"Dad! If he pulls in the same direction, but at a slightly different angle, those sidewalls will give way," George shouted.

Pete looked at the elevator, then back at George, and then ran over toward the bulldozer waving his bandaged hand like a white flag for Harold to stop.

They conferred for a minute and then Pete waved George over to drag the cables back again. The whole time, George kept an eye on the building in case it decided to get even with them and fall over early.

This time Harold took up the slack at about half-speed. As it tightened, he stomped the throttle forward as far as it would go and held it there.

The cable snapped into a straight line, and then vibrated as if strummed.

The building seemed to twist slightly and then both sides gave way just as George predicted.

The bulldozer seemed to leap ahead momentarily.

The elevator came down very fast with pistol-shots sounds, and a cracking, deafening groan. Then it landed with an explosion of dust and debris.

Harold disappeared in the billowing cloud.

The ground shook and vibrated.

The noise continued, thunderous, drowning out the engine noise and everything else. Later, Harold found dents in his barn-roofing shield. He hadn't even heard anything hit it. "The hell! It didn't seem like D8 was going fast enough to get me clear. I nearly shit my pants."

The cloud of dust enveloped half the town, but the wind spared the other half, the more fortunate half. The rest of the dust didn't settle for an hour.

George and Pete were busy dragging pieces off the street and never thought about what they looked like. George happened to look over and saw that Pete looked like a photo negative, all black with a white background. He started laughing. Pete looked over at him and then he started laughing too. Harold heard them, looked over, and had a good laugh as well, but he was still clean.

"It just goes to show you who's doing all the work around here," Pete said. George happened to look back across the street, behind him. The redheaded girl was standing there covered with dirt, too. When she saw George looking at her, she ran off.

Then the real work began. All three of them began prying large sections loose from the tumbled-down walls. They had to use a sledgehammer and wedges to get each section started before using alternating crowbars to finish their pry. Then Harold started the truck and the three of them used it to drag large chunks down off the railroad and out of the street. Afterwards, Pete inspected the tracks and pronounced them undamaged.

Pete pried individual two-by-sixes loose and built a ramp up onto the bed of the truck. Again, he used nails pulled from the elevator walls. Harold had already rigged up a hand-crank winch and pulley system he had salvaged from an old wrecker to pull them up onto the truck bed. Once they had the truck loaded with all it could hold, Harold and Pete hauled the sections home to unload.

George stayed and worked on the lumber until 5:00 O'clock. He got to drive Harold's car home at the end of the day. He was excited to drive such a big fancy car. It was a 1948 Kaiser Custom Sedan and Harold kept it in like new condition. As he was leaving, he saw the redheaded girl again. Clean. She waved at him and he waved back.

Harold's wife kept him home for the Sabbath the next day, but Pete and George took Harold's truck back for another load. They were finished by noon and George found out how easy it was to unload.

Harold had leased a fallow field just down the road to store the lumber. They worked the two-inch rope down and around as many sections as they could, tied the other end to a big tree on the fence line and drove away in granny gear. More than half of the load came off in a single pull.

Pete said, "There's a million nails sticking out of the bottoms, holding them together. Be damned careful around those rusty nails. And for God's sake, and for your mother's, don't step on one."

Their method spread the pieces over a wide area, but it made them easier to work. On weekdays, George and Harold worked the site of the elevator together, tearing loose and loading as much as they could. There was a lot of lumber. Harold had other irons in the fire though and once or twice a week he would leave George there alone to pry smaller sections apart.

The first day that he was alone, George took a break for lunch and sought shade behind a large section of wall. He was sitting with his back to the wall, knees propped up, eating a bacon, lettuce and biscuit sandwich, when the red-haired girl came around the corner. She was wearing a white, sleeveless, knee-length dress with a Peter Pan collar and brown, canvas, low-cut shoes. Her ankles were bare. The dress was patterned with faded, small blue flowers.

He jumped to his feet and she stopped in her tracks. They stared at each other for a moment and then she held out a flour sack. "I thought you might like some ice tea and a piece of pie."

"Thank you. Have a seat, but watch out for nails." He gestured toward a smaller section at right angles to the one he was using. He took the bag and peered inside. He had two biscuit sandwiches and a jug of water, but no pie or tea. The tea was in a glass-quart milk jug with a foil on top, held in place by a rubber band.

She sat watching him while he ate and he smiled at her while he chewed. "What's your name?" he asked.

"Crystal. What's yours?"

"Hi Crystal, I'm George." He didn't beat around the bush. "How old are you Crystal?"

"Fifteen."

"You sure don't look it."

"I'll be in tenth grade when school starts."

He was silent for a while, eating a fried pie, his first one ever. He thought, *she sure is cute with her curly, red hair and light freckles.* When he finished, he said, "Thank you. It was delicious. Peach is my favorite, but I never tasted anything like that before. Did you make it?

"No, my ma did. It's a fried pie."

For the first time, George noticed her southern accent. "Where are you from Crystal? Sounds like the South."

"Bearden, Arkansas." Before he could ask where that was, she said, "Over t'other side of Pine Bluff. Ain't nobody ever heard of Bearden. Ain't much there."

George shrugged, "Well, I ain't never been to Arkansas anyway. So, how'd you get up here?"

"My daddy came up the rivers fishin. He heard there was great big fish up North. He drownded in the Kankakee River last year, so we're stuck here."

"That's terrible," George said——at a loss for anything else to say.

They sat there for a couple more minutes, and then she said, "You're sitting in the shade but I'm gettin burnt out here in the sun. Can I move over by you?"

"OK, but I can't sit here long. I've got to get back to work."

Crystal moved over and sat by George, too close for his comfort, close enough to feel her body heat. She sure is small, he thought, but shapely too.

He asked her about school and she said that she had to take two buses and went to Hanna. He doubted that she would be bussed that far but didn't say anything. He felt antsy being that close to her and not knowing that much about her, so he said, "I've got to get back to work."

She jumped to her feet and said, "I'll come back next time I see you." As she left, he admired the motion of her small hips and the way the sun shone through the light dress.

George worked with Harold for a week and only saw Crystal from a distance. The following week Harold let him drive the truck there alone, but he didn't see her until lunch time. Again, she showed up, but with a paper sack, the jug separate. She was dressed the same but this time the dress was pale yellow with the faded blue flowers. She sat down beside him without asking, and handed him the bag. "Apple with raisins this time."

He grinned, put his arm around her, and gave her a little hug. She clasped her hands tightly between her knees. She leaned into the hug slightly, but stayed stiff as a board.

George released her and opened the bag. He took a whiff then closed it back up. "I'm going to eat my sandwich first. You want a squirrel sandwich?"

"What? I've eaten plenty of squirrel, but never in a sandwich."

"I was just kidding, Crystal. It's pork sausage. My neighbor makes it."

"Let me try a bite." She did, and said, "Oh, that's good. Do you have enough? He handed it over and then unwrapped another. She finished hers before he was halfway through. He thought she must have really been hungry. Then it dawned on him. The pie and tea were probably *her* lunch.

"I'm glad you remembered my name, George."

"Where do you live, Crystal?"

"Back yonder," she said pointing to the poorer side of town. That area of town consisted of two old, dilapidated cracker-box houses and some run-down shacks. Much like Papertown, he thought.

Crystal slid right up against him, so he put his arm around her and kissed her. She was willing for the kiss but was all tensed up. She held her lips tightly closed and pushed them hard against his. He was sure she hadn't kissed anyone before, and he pulled away.

"I asked around about you Crystal, You're only twelve."

"Nuh-uh! I'm 13." Her hand flew to her mouth. She knew she'd been tricked.

"Crystal, you are really nice and very pretty, but you are way too young for me. You'd better go now."

Tears welled up in her eyes. "You boys just want for yourselves," she said as she turned and ran.

"I'm sorry Crystal," he shouted. "You forgot your milk jug." But she was gone. He walked across the street and set the jug on the raised concrete curb.

By the end of that weekend, they finished loading and picked up all the debris. The job in Dent was finished and he wondered if he would ever see Crystal again. When they got there the last day, he noticed that the milk jug was gone.

The work prying the lumber apart and pulling nails in the field kept him busy and away from Papertown for the rest of the summer. Harold was selling used lumber, either cleaned with no nails, or dirty with nails. George was surprised at how many people bought the lumber with the nails still in it, but not enough of them to get it all gone.

The sections were scattered and that allowed him room to work. He sorted each size by length, resulting in several stacks spaced above ground with crosspieces. The crosspieces kept the stack from drawing moisture from the ground.

He had to wait on Harold for help prying the big sections apart. With all of the different piles and stacks, the area became a maze. Then, tired, he jumped down from a three-foot high section and landed on a nail. His dad had warned not to leave any boards on the ground with the nails sticking up.

The nail poked clear up through his right foot, just above and to one side of the ball, and stuck up half-an-inch, shining red. He stood there, not moving for a few seconds, jumbled thoughts running through his head. He was surprised at himself, that he hadn't hollered, that he had gotten careless, and he knew the pain would be coming. He knew what he had to do.

George yanked his foot straight up off the nail, yelling out as he did so, and hobbled home the quarter-mile distance walking on the heel of his right foot. He never noticed that he'd left his shirt behind.

Pete and Lois Rickson drove their son to a doctor in town, who gave him a tetanus shot. Pete's only admonishment was, "Well, I guess the pain is your lesson. There's more of that to come, but you will be back out there working tomorrow."

The doctor proclaimed that his foot had suffered no permanent damage.

When they got home George's parents made him soak his foot in a dishpan full of hot water and Epsom salts until the water cooled down. The pain of the hot water was greater than the pain from the nail and the shot. George thought it was going to take his skin off. He yelped when his foot first hit the water and he saw a smirk on Pete's face.

He did go back to work on the lumber the next afternoon, and soaked his foot again that night, and the next, but George was sick of pulling the 16 and 20-penny spikes. The nails were his to keep for scrap iron, but it seemed to take forever to fill up a five-gallon bucket with them. His plan was to save enough money to buy a car.

During that period, he never saw Carrie or any of the Papertown kids. He missed Carrie. He occasionally thought about little Crystal and hoped she would be all right. He was afraid the wrong guy would come along and take advantage of her.

CHAPTER 23

That winter was the longest and coldest that anyone in the area could remember. It was exceptionally difficult for people who had little or nothing to sustain them through the long periods of cold and snow. By the first week of January, snow covered the ground at a depth of eighteen inches or more on the level, higher than floor level on the Papertown shacks and the Rickson house.

The weather was unrelenting for the following month also, with only more wind keeping the snow from getting even deeper on open, level ground. The new accumulation piled up in drifts, some as high as sixteen feet, drifting over some of the doorways in Papertown. People without a solid door on their shacks propped a mattress up in the doorway.

Almost constant winds created whiteouts that restricted virtually all movement of man, animal or machine, and below-zero temperatures caused some items in the shacks to freeze. In one shack, canned goods on a corner shelf froze and broke their Mason jars. In most of them, a blanket was stretched across a corner to conceal a pot, or bucket used as a pot. The pot was for those unable to go outside to relieve themselves. Real pots were metal with a flanged top and a matching lid. Most were white with a baked-on enamel or porcelain finish and had a decorative stripe or pattern around the top. With the blanket isolating what little heat there was in the room, the corner pots froze too. Some said this was a blessing in disguise.

Someone forgot to let the outdoor community pump down after getting water and the pump froze solid, cutting off the water supply. Men tried building a fire around it with some of the precious firewood. When the fire got hot enough to start melting ice around the pump, they discovered the pipe had split just below it. The joint was under the frozen ground, making repairs impossible for the time being.

The fire also burned the washtub stand under the pump. From then on snow was melted in the shacks in boiler kettles or buckets on the flimsy stoves. Occasionally someone made it to the Rickson' or Schmidt' houses for water.

The supply of usable firewood in Papertown was running out and residents were forced to move in with others to conserve what little was left. Even then, they began sacrificing anything burnable they could do without. One by one, different items disappeared. First it was the magazines and catalogs, then orange-crate storage furniture and wooden toys. Later people were breaking up their manufactured furniture and burning old shoes. People gave up what few wooden bed frames existed. Headboards, footboards and bed-slats were all turned into fuel.

In some of the shacks with more than one family in them, mattresses covered the floors wall-to-wall on one side and halfway across on the other. Clothes, with no bureaus, dressers or boxes to contain them, piled up on the mattresses to isolate people and to help cover them. Clothes hanging from nails covered the walls. Some people slept in shifts from the shortage of beds.

A few residents braved the elements just long enough to drag seats and backs from automobiles into the shacks to use for sitting or sleeping. Fights started constantly from the close proximity, forcing some of the combatants out into the cold, but their antagonists accepted then back in almost immediately to keep them from freezing to death.

Some who ventured outdoors during the sub-zero temperatures paid dearly. More than one person got frostbite on their toes or fingers. One man got gangrene in two toes and had his neighbor chop them off with a hatchet to keep the poison from getting into his bloodstream.

Later he said, "I couldn't feel a damned thing in those toes before they were taken off, but I sure as hell felt pain in them after they were gone, and lots of it."

Winter wore on.

By the second week of March, the snow and wind had stopped but temperatures were still below freezing. As people and traffic began moving again, word of another tragedy in the area reached Papertown. A couple from town had stopped by the James Farm on the next road back hoping to buy eggs, milk and pickled ham. They found a cold, dark and silent house. After pounding on the front door for a while, they discovered the back door was unlocked, so they entered.

Inside they found the body of Mrs. James. It was huddled wrapped in blankets on the floor beside the bed. The coroner had to move the frozen body in its fetal position, blankets and all, to the county morgue. After the body thawed out, it was discovered she had a broken hip and pelvis, apparently from an earlier fall. The Sheriff and the coroner agreed that she was alone in the house and that all of the firewood had been burned. Unable to crawl up onto the bed, she had pulled all the bedclothes down onto herself in her efforts to stay warm.

The Jameses didn't have a telephone. Mr. James had been heard to refer to a telephone as a "new-fangled nuisance." They searched outside but couldn't find him.

Sheriff Parks had noticed the sealed-off upstairs and was puzzled by it. He couldn't imagine Mrs. James locking her husband up there unless he was laying up there dead. He didn't think she would have been capable of nailing the door shut and climbing a ladder to seal off the register anyway. There was no ladder in the house and when he looked closer, he noted that the door had been painted-over long before. Despite his misgivings, he sent a deputy for crowbars or ripping bars, reasoning that someone else might be up there.

"James may have gotten lost in a whiteout, or maybe even had a heart attack. He's probably under a snow-bank out there somewhere," the Sheriff said while waiting.

When the deputy arrived, they pried away the strips nailed around the door, but the old paint held fast. With chisels and knives, they cut away at the paint sealing the cracks. Then, by prying all around it, they finally got it open, gouging and splintering both door and frame around the edges. It came open with a screech and they were greeted with a blast of icy-cold, stale air with a slightly pungent smell of decay.

The upstairs contained two bedrooms and a small door leading into an attic. The bedroom at the top of the stairs was completely empty with not so much as a single toothpick or a mouse turd in evidence.

The attic was full of discarded household and shop items and junk of bygone days. The other bedroom had another closed, sealed door and they went through the pry-bar process again. The surprise lay inside.

The desiccated body of a young boy, fully clothed in a small suit, flat cap, necktie and shoes, lay on top of a quilted, made bed. A single, dusty sheet covered him from head to toe. "He was maybe four or five years old. No telling how many years he's laid up here... at least long enough for the smell to have dissipated," the sheriff said. He felt around the back of the head and the neck, and then around the body, rolling it from side to side without undressing it. It gave off a musty smell and made a slight crunching noise when he moved it, like dried, stiff leather. Motes of dust from fabric or skin rose from it and danced in the streaks of sunlight filtering through the single, dirty window. "It looks like he died of natural causes, but the coroner will have to determine that."

Sheriff Parks surveyed the room, taking in the fact that it had been a boy's room with coats and jackets hanging on pegs from the shiny, yellow walls. A chest of drawers held other clothes for a small boy. Shelves held books and toys. He noticed a couple of *Uncle Remus* books. Shoes and boots lined up neatly in a row under the edge of the bed. He was confident that the boy had lived in that house and that this was his room.

The James couple had lived there longer than anyone else had been around the area, including the sheriff himself. He inquired later on and found that no one could remember them ever having a child. Word spread from one of the deputies who had been there, to his brother who worked at the sawmill. From there it quickly made its way back to Papertown and the Ricksons.

It was two more weeks before anyone found out what had happened to Mr. James. Most of the snow had finally melted, leaving a muddy quagmire around the farmhouse and outbuildings.

Resuming the search, the Sheriff noticed a broken top-board at the hog lot fence. The main part of the hog lot consisted of woven-wire fence, but the section extending from the side of the barn was made from slabwood. This section was used as a feeding area, or to hem the hogs up for loading. Now, as he approached the hog lot, he noticed that the hogs were gone. Looking out over the lot Sheriff Parks saw a boot lying on the ground at the back corner of the barn. He crawled in to investigate and found the boot still had a foot in it, with lower leg bones attached, half of the flesh gone. The bone had not been visible from his vantage point at the corner of the barn.

Further investigation revealed more bones and the deflated looking bib overalls that all farmers wore. This and a coat were shredded and almost invisible in the mire. At the back of the hog lot was a hole in the bottom of the woven-wire fence. The most gruesome discovery was the skull with the face partially eaten away. It had been rooted into the corner by the hogs.

The inquest determined that Mr. James must have fallen into the hog lot when a board broke while he was feeding them.

Sheriff Parks said, "He must have sustained sufficient injury not to have immediately regained his feet. Hogs won't eat carrion, but they will attack and eat an injured or bleeding animal of any species, especially when hungry or starving." His words were taken as a portion of the grand jury's verdict.

The official coroner's condensed version was "*Attacked and killed by animals while injured from a fall.*"

Later, people discovered the hogs in the woods. They and some of the other livestock had somehow survived. Area residents hunted down and killed all the hogs they could find. Some were butchered, roasted and eaten by Papertown residents while others refused to eat the meat, saying; "You might be eating part of Old Man James."

George stayed out of Papertown for the rest of the winter and didn't participate in the hog hunts.

CHAPTER 24

That spring George turned sixteen and looked more like a man than a boy. "A handsome man," some of the women in Papertown were saying. George's parents sensed a restlessness in him, and knew he needed something they couldn't provide, something that was beyond their reach. He heard his dad say, "I don't know what to do with him mother." If she answered, George never heard her.

The next day, His dad told him that it was time for him to get himself a regular job, and that he would have to get it on his own. He said, "I'll help you get a car but you'll have to pay for it from your own earnings. If you don't pay, I'll take it back."

That sounded good enough to George, He had already spent all of his earnings from Harold on magazines, soda pop, snacks and some mail-order tools. His dad had never given him any money from their share of the elevator business. He didn't know when or how much he would get, if he ever got any at all.

He had first learned to drive a car from his Uncle Ward two years before. They had started lessons in a cow pasture with Ward's old 47 Chevy.

It had a three-speed, column shift and George wasn't aware that there was any other kind of shift for cars. He had also driven Harold Schmidt's 1948 Kaiser Custom Sedan, with a column shift. He knew about floor shifts in trucks, though, having driven the Diamond T.

He'd asked his dad about having Ward's car, but his dad looked at him stone-faced and said, "Wards missing, not dead. Don't ask again."

The car they found for George was an old Chrysler with a Gyromatic transmission. The shift was on the column but operated differently, not requiring use of the clutch for the higher gears. They bought the car from a skinny, toothless old farmer named Floyd Hames for fifty dollars. The car was to stay at the Hames' farm until George paid the entire fifty dollars. George was allowed to make improvements on the car during that time, but that was all. During the search for the car he found out about *Powerglide* in the newer model Chevy he wanted, but didn't get.

His dad said, "A man doesn't often get exactly what he wants Son, but makes what he gets fit himself and his needs."

The matter was closed. The bad part was that the car didn't run. George would have to pay for it, figure out what was wrong with it himself, and fix it himself. He wouldn't be driving it for a while. He knew that times were hard and his dad was barely hanging on to his own job. He wasn't about to mention the money he had taken from Mr. Corbett's wallet. It was still hidden under the house and he thought that someday he would give it to Annie McDews, even though he didn't know where she lived.

He did understand about not having money though. He had stood in the food lines with some of the Papertown people to help them carry home their allotments of government surplus cheese, butter and powdered milk, as well as the day-old-bread and skim milk from the government issued chits. Though the Ricksons weren't poor, things weren't all that good. Some of the issued items usually found their way to their home in exchange for items George's dad could barter from others. George liked the butter and cheese, but thought the powdered milk was awful.

Occasionally there was a train wreck or derailment. One occurred that spring. A dump truck driver with a load of gravel tried to beat the train while maneuvering across an angled crossing. His passenger-side rear wheels ran off the crossing ties and his axle hung up. His five-yard dump truck was hit at the right rear of the fully loaded dump bed. The train was only going forty miles-per-hour but the weight of the load in the truck caused an impact that not only spun the truck around and tipped it over onto its side, but derailed the train as well.

The truck driver stayed in the cab and was only skinned up. His load spilled onto the road, blocking it behind him. The engineer and fireman in the train were severely injured from being slammed into the levers and the firebox. The engine and coal car remained upright, but several boxcars following them overturned.

Among the items in the rail cars were packaged foods, canned goods, fertilizer and a boxcar full of shoes. Bulldozers were brought in from a radius of fifty miles to clean up the mess.

Railroad officials allowed private citizens to carry off perishables, such as canned goods and packaged foods but no one was allowed to take items such as shoes, farm equipment or fertilizer.

Despite the rules, almost everyone in Papertown got one or two pairs of new shoes that year. George's dad wouldn't allow any of the shoes in his house, he worked for the railroad. They did get canned goods and cereal though. It wasn't long before George was sick of canned carrots, spinach, and *Post Toasties*. He was glad for the Papertown residents, though.

CHAPTER 25

George was sitting on his back-porch steps one sunny Saturday morning, admiring the morning glories curling up near his feet and the early morning quiet. He heard a dull thud from Papertown and then some faint scuffling noises. Rising from the porch, he quietly walked toward the shacks, not wanting to wake anyone.

Normally this early on a weekend morning, no one was awake. When George got among the shacks, the noises were louder. The sounds were coming from between two shacks near the outhouse on the end. As he drew closer, he could distinguish the thudding of feet in the dirt and hear hissing sounds. Then he heard a louder thud, like a chunk of firewood slamming against the side of a shack.

When he peered around the corner, the sight of two grown women fighting startled him. One of them was Elsie Jones, a mildly pretty woman around thirty. She had blue eyes and thick, short dark hair with bangs in front. The back hung straight across at the base of her neck, framing her sharp features. Her skin looked like it was stretched over her cheekbones though, giving her somewhat of a hard look around the eyes.

The other woman was Pansy Barnett, an attractive strawberry blonde with a few childhood acne scars that only showed up in direct sunlight. Pansy was older but still very shapely. George had guessed her to be about forty.

The women struggled in a face-to-face battle between the shacks. Both of them wore thin cotton, short-sleeved, knee-length dresses with no collars. Pansy had a grip on Elsie's hair with both hands, twisting her head from side-to-side trying rip it out. Elsie had the neckline of Pansy's dress in both hands, with her wrists crossed, trying to choke her with it. They struggled in a circle, kicking at each other and hissing through their teeth from their exertion. Elsie was barefooted and favoring one leg as she hopped around. George noticed the front of Pansy's leg was bloody and she was wearing clodhopper shoes. Both of them were medium-height, rawboned women and appeared about evenly matched. Suddenly, Elsie bit into Pansy's forearm during the struggle.

Pansy let out a yell and swung Elsie bodily into the wall of the nearest shack. Elsie lost her bite-hold, and as she bounced back, Pansy, who hadn't lost her grip on Elsie's hair, head-butted her on the nose. Up to that point, Elsie had drawn blood from Pansy twice. Now, it sprayed from Elsie's face and covered both of them from neck to chest. Elsie's legs buckled and she nearly fell, but she didn't lose her grip on Pansy's dress until it ripped open nearly to the waist.

They both lost their holds then and staggered backwards. Pansy had pulled out a handful of Elsie's hair but one of her own breasts had flopped out into the open, soon followed by the other. George stood watching from only a few feet away but wasn't about to interfere. It looked like a good way to get clawed, bitten or kicked. Neither of the women was aware of him and he wasn't aware of Mr. Schmidt either.

Harold Schmidt yelled out, "Stop it!" as he stepped past George toward the women. George laid a hand on his arm and said, "Wait, they'll just start again later if they don't get it settled now. Besides, I'd rather stick my hand in a bag of wildcats."

Schmidt hesitated as the women launched themselves at each other again. Elsie had both blood and tears running down her face but still spotted the exposed breasts of Pansy in front of her. With a shriek, she clawed at them with fingernails extended.

Pansy, who had been distracted by Mr. Schmidt's yell, now yelled too, "Stealing bitch, I'll put you in hell!" She swung a fist into Elsie's eye.

Elsie staggered sideways, but on her recovery, tackled Pansy, grabbing her around the neck and one shoulder. Again, she kicked at Pansy's legs with her toenails. Pansy was trying to twist away and both of them lost their balance and went down. They rolled over and over in the dirt from one shack to the next, hissing and spitting and trying to stab each other in the eyes with their fingernails. Pansy, on the bottom, managed to grab a handful of dirt and throw it into Elsie's eyes, causing her to roll away.

"We've got to stop them before they kill each other," Mr. Schmidt said.

Pansy had rolled over on top while Elsie was wiping at her eyes with one hand. Mr. Schmidt grabbed her from behind and pulled her up from Elsie. As she was coming up, she took the opportunity to launch a kick to Elsie's jaw with her clodhopper shoe. The kick snapped Elsie's head halfway around and knocked her senseless.

Now, Pansy turned on her captor who hadn't realized he'd accidentally grabbed her by the bare breasts when he pulled her free. She turned in his grasp, clawed at his face and stomped on his instep with her heavy shoe. George took the opportunity to grab her around the throat from behind, while locking her right arm in a half-nelson. She was nearly as tall as George and reached over her shoulder trying to twist him around her back and over her hip. He couldn't believe how strong she was.

This gave Mr. Schmidt a chance to step back in and get a better hold. He grabbed both of her hands and yelled in her face, "It's over. She's dead!"

Pansy stopped her struggles and seemed to wilt in George's arms. She slid down his legs to a sitting position and burst into tears with loud hiccups before he could free his arms. Her dress rode up her thighs, exposing her shapely legs, and George noticed sunlight glistening on the reddish-blonde hairs on her shins as he pulled his arms away. He stood there for a minute looking down over her shoulder while letting her use his legs for a backrest. She folded her arms across her chest and he looked away, ashamed at what he was thinking. He noticed Mr. Schmidt looking away red faced too.

Elsie wasn't dead, but still hadn't been able to get to her feet. She was trying to crawl away without seeming to know what she was crawling away from or where she was crawling to. They left her there while they got Pansy back on her feet and led her to the Schmidt house.

Pansy was saying, "I caught her stealing out of my purse right in my own house."

She was holding the top of her dress together with both hands now and seemed oblivious to the people around her. She was bleeding from both legs below the knee and from the bite on her arm. It looked like her face was swollen but George couldn't tell for sure because of all the dirt. She had been taking in washings since Annie McDews left, and her hands always looked red and chapped around the knuckles. He noticed now that one of her knuckles was split.

Pansy and Clovis had three kids, with Pootie being the middle child. Lenny the youngest, was nine. Henry, the oldest at eighteen, had joined the Navy. He finished boot camp at Great Lakes in Illinois and was now at Memphis, Tennessee.

George was surprised at how firm her body had felt in his arms and how nice her breasts looked before Elsie had clawed at them. He wondered what the scars would look like, if she got any. He also noticed that there were several adults in different stages of dress watching, and kids peering around the corners of the shacks. He felt himself blush from what he'd been thinking. No one, other than Pansy, had said a word since Mr. Schmidt had said Elsie was dead.

They left Pansy on the Schmidt steps for Mrs. Schmidt and other women to attend to, and returned for Elsie. She had gotten to her feet but was now in the grasp of the much larger Esther Wales. Esther had her pinned to the wall of the Barnett shack with one big hand spread in a V around her throat. With the other, she had a big, pink, freckled fist cocked back as if to deliver a blow to Elsie's bloody, bruised and dirty face. Elsie wasn't moving and her swollen eyes were rolling around like a trapped animal. George doubted that she would be able to see out of either one by the next day.

"You steal my gold watch and my three dollars?" Esther shouted in her face. There were blotchy, bright-red spots on her neck and face. Everyone knew Esther was serious.

Elsie was slowly moving her head from side to side. Whether it was a negative answer or whether she was trying to focus, was unclear.

Esther slugged her in the stomach instead, and then let her fall. She turned her back and headed away before anyone could object. George was glad, because he sure didn't want to tangle with Esther.

Elsie was lying doubled over on her side on the ground, dry heaving and trying to get her breath. No one seemed inclined to help her.

She and her husband Jesse didn't have any kids and neither socialized much. He worked in a tavern over at the county seat, bartending, handling stock and empties and cleaning up in the after-hours. They were up when most Papertown residents were sleeping and sleeping during the middle of the day. Talk was that he poured the dregs from the nearly empty liquor bottles into a flask and carried the mix home with him. The few people who accepted a drink from him did so only once.

There was always some minor theft going on in Papertown, but there had been recent rumors of someone stealing money, clothes and jewelry from the shacks on a regular basis. George knew that the money would have been small amounts and that the jewelry would have more sentimental value than monetary value. He couldn't imagine anyone in there really having enough to make the risk worthwhile. Now he heard a commotion farther down the line and realized Esther had entered the Joneses' shack.

There was a howl from Jesse Jones, who awoke to find Esther looming over him and others entering the shack behind her. George and Harold Schmidt were close enough to distinguish words.

"What the hell's going on?" Jesse bellowed from his bed.

Jesse told people that he was half-Indian and he had the features to match with straight black hair, a prominent nose, imperceptible beard and sunken dark eyes. His skin was lily-white, though.

Esther glared back down at him. "Get out of that bed. You and your woman's been stealing from all of us. Now you're going to show us where it's at."

George and Mr. Schmidt got to the door just in time to see her reach for the blanket covering his lower half and see him kick out. Jesse was a good-sized man and had a grip on the bedrail with his left hand. His heel caught her on the inside of the right knee. As big as she was, George heard the knee pop and she went down on her hind end and elbows like a lightning-struck tree, shaking the whole shack when she hit the floor. She let out a screech and started scrabbling backwards with her right hand, left elbow and left foot before anyone else could react. Her left hand still clutched the corner of Jesse's blanket, pulling it completely off the bed.

"You done broke my leg you moron!" she screamed.

"Serves you right," exclaimed Billy Allen's mom, Patricia.

George knew that if Esther hadn't been disabled, Patricia wouldn't have said that.

"What do you mean coming into a man's house like this?" Jesse jumped out of bed completely naked, causing a couple of the women to gasp at his larger-than-average hardware. Even the now moaning Esther took a good look.

At the same time another woman said, "Here's my missing towels and them's my bloomers." She had pulled open a drawer on an old wallpaper-covered buffet and was rummaging through it.

Others stepped over to it and one of the women said, "I've been missing my Virgil's drawers and here they are."

"I've been missing money," said a man from the door.

Jesse had been about to make a grab for the nearest woman when he heard the man's voice. It suddenly dawned on him that he was naked in front of several people with men coming after him.

"Stop!" he yelled. "Let me get my pants on and we'll get to the bottom of this."

"OK! Everybody else out, except George," Schmidt hollered. He grabbed a woman by the wrist as she was trying to leave with a watch and necklace in her hands. "Everything stays here until everyone has had a look and a say."

"Why the kid?" someone asked.

"Because he works for me and he's neutral," said Schmidt. "I can trust him," he added.

After everyone was out and someone had loaded Esther into a car to haul her to the hospital, things calmed down. Once Jesse heard what it was all about, he agreed to let people come into the shack one at a time to go through their boxes and the buffet, with Mr. Schmidt as arbitrator. He swore he didn't know anything had been stolen. His story and cooperation were believable. No one except the Wales family blamed him for kicking out at Esther, even if it did break her leg. Opinion was that she was a big bully, the same as a man.

More money was found than the amount claimed to have been stolen. Later Elsie admitted to hoarding household money by stealing instead of buying. She wanted to leave Jesse because of his drinking, and felt she needed money to do it. Some didn't blame her and Jesse threw her out that day, anyway.

Jesse stayed and George could tell that some of the women didn't mind this at all, especially those who had been in the shack when he jumped out of bed naked.

George went with Mr. Schmidt to drive Elsie to the county seat where she could catch a bus. She made a half-hearted play for Mr. Schmidt that might have been more serious if George hadn't been along and she hadn't been in such poor shape from the beating.

It didn't matter though; Harold Schmidt wasn't interested. He let her keep half of the overage from the money count to get started, and gave her a few more dollars to help with the bus trip. She had some healing to do before she could be serious about attracting another husband and she would always have a crooked nose.

George thought of Pansy and the serious scars she would have on her legs, arm and maybe other places. George also thought about Annie McDews and wondered how much different life would be if he knew what had happened to her and her kids.

Before long, George would meet a different kind of woman.

CHAPTER 26

Other than Frank Yount, George had always gotten along well with his teachers. With the start of his sophomore year, all of them were new to him, as were most of the students. The county bussed the other students in from adjacent townships.

His ninth grade English teacher, Mrs. Krass, had counseled him to take typing and Latin before graduating. "You will need them both to further your education. Even if you don't go to college, they will both help you with other things in life."

The next year, he signed up for typing but decided to wait until his senior year before committing to Latin.

His typing teacher, Miss Noonan, was the youngest teacher he'd ever had. She was small and shapeless, with mousey, shoulder-length brown hair. She wore thick glasses and no makeup and it gave her heart-shaped face a bland, owl-eyed look. When she stood behind George's chair to check his finger positions, he noticed that she smelled like a pleasant soap, rather than perfume.

George struggled with the typing. It seemed to him that the keys should be in alphabetical order. He told Miss Noonan that while she was standing at his left shoulder, and she laughed. So did the rest of the class, embarrassing him.

"You are right, George. The keys were originally in alphabetical order. Now they are actually laid out to slow down a fast typist so that the keys don't jam. Let me sit in your chair for a minute." She turned toward the class. "All right class, gather around." She started a new sheet of paper in the typewriter.

In a minute, the class surrounded them. "OK George. Talk to me."

At first, he didn't know what to say, then he came out with, "Four score and seven years ago our fathers brought forth upon this continent a new nation." He stopped there.

When he stopped speaking, Miss Noonan stopped typing and said, "Something else."

Another student, a girl, started quoting the 23rd Psalm. Others picked up on it, quoting different subjects. As they spoke, Miss Noonan typed. Her fingers were a blur on the keys. The sound of the levers hitting the ribbon-stop sounded like a machine gun. When they paused or stopped talking, she instantly stopped typing.

When her page was full, she stopped and pulled the sheet from the typewriter. She handed it to George and said, "Pass it around."

She had kept up, and typed every word they said. He didn't see any errors. The class was in awe, silent as each one read it and returned to their seats.

She stood close to George as she spoke. He noticed that she had the straightest and whitest teeth he had ever seen. She patted him on the shoulder as she walked away. "You will be all right in this class, George." When George sat back down, the seat felt hot.

Later, she stopped by and leaned over him to look at the paper he was typing. She straightened without a word and walked on to check someone else's work.

Where her hand had rested on his desk was a small, folded square of paper. He unfolded it and read, *please stop by my desk after class, MN.* He only had five minutes between classes, so he knew that whatever she wanted wouldn't take long.

When he approached her desk at the end of the session, she was looking at one of his pages. "Look at this, George." He stepped around the corner of her desk, past the visitor chair, so he could look over her shoulder. She continued, "You are being too cautious. Don't worry so much about errors and you will pick up speed." While George listened, she continued. "George, I've been told that you read a lot of books. Would you be interested in joining a book club?"

As she talked, he noticed that her feet were wrapped around the chair legs, ankles on the outside, toes on the inside. She seemed to be squeezing the legs of the chair. He thought *that means something.* He wasn't sure what though. Maybe she was just nervous.

"Well, maybe," he answered.

"Come back by my classroom after school lets out and I will tell you more about it."

"I only have about ten minutes to catch my bus."

"I'll make sure you don't miss your bus, George." He noticed that she used his name when she talked to him.

When he entered the room after school, she gestured toward the chair at the side of her desk. "George, I host a book club twice a month. We read through a classic or modern best seller and discuss the finer points as we progress.

"There are a dozen members but usually only three or four show up. Two of the regulars are teachers and one of those is Barnes, your mechanical drawing teacher. The others are just local people who like to read. You would be the only student."

"Well, I don't know how I could do that. I live too far to walk home. Where is it held?"

"The meetings are at my house and I know about where you live. I'm sure we can find you a ride home. And, it's only a couple times a month."

"Yes. Let me talk to my parents, but I think it will be all right. I'd like to try it."

"Okay, George. Let me know. The next meeting is this coming Tuesday."

Both parents agreed, thinking it would help keep him out of trouble. His mom especially was proud of her son, standing-out at school. "How will you get your supper?" she asked.

"Can you pack me a double lunch?"

"What time is the meeting?"

"She told me that it starts at 6:00 and lasts until 8:00 or 9:00."

"How are you going to get there and get home?" his dad asked.

"She lives in town, so I can walk there. She said that one of them would drive me home."

"Good. I'm up too early in the morning to go get you that late at night."

The next day was Friday, so he told Miss Noonan that he would be able to go.

"I'm glad George. If you can hang around half-an-hour after school on Tuesday, I'll give you a ride. We are reading and discussing Ian Fleming's *Casino Royale*. You can get a copy in the school library."

George was surprised on both counts, but the half-hour would give him time to eat first. "I can walk," he said.

"I don't think so, George. I live halfway between here and Papertown."

"Oh, you know about Papertown?"

"I know you live nearby."

"Okay," said George, "I'll be glad for the ride."

The book wasn't available at the school library and he had to walk to the public library for it. The same day he checked out the book, he began reading it. He was really looking forward to discussing books with adults. None of the kids in his neighborhood read books. His mother read one occasionally, but not something that he would read.

Tuesday evening, Miss Noonan picked him up at the front of the school when nearly everyone else was gone. She was driving a clean-looking, 1949, light-green Plymouth. When he got in, he noticed that she was sitting on a pillow with another one behind her back. However, she drove with skill and confidence.

As usual, she was wearing a loose, gray-print skirt that draped to her ankles. She had her white blouse buttoned nearly to her throat.

"So, how long have you been reading adult books, George?"

"Oh, probably since I was twelve or thirteen."

"That's good. You will go far in life. Now what we do is, between meetings, we read one or two chapters, depending on how long they are, and then discuss them at the next meeting. That is why I asked you to read the first two, so you would be caught up with us."

She drove in silence for a few minutes, staring at the road. Then she glanced over at him. "George, I don't want you to be embarrassed, but we eat at my house. It's sort of a finger-food potluck. We don't expect you to bring anything, though. We are thrilled to have younger people read."

"I'm looking forward to it. The book is already interesting."

Miss Noonan's house was a small, cedar-sided house, painted white. It was at the end of a dead-end street halfway to Papertown. The street was part of a small subdivision just north of the intersection of the state highway and the county-line road.

She turned in at a driveway and parked in a small garage attached to the house by a breezeway. The double, hinged doors were propped open. The bare, unpainted inside walls were decorated with only a few garden tools. A single shelf at the far end held automotive fluids, yard and garden chemicals and a fly sprayer.

As they exited the car, she said, "This was my grandmother's house. I inherited it."

Inside, the house was tastefully, but not expensively, decorated. She had prepared and refrigerated small sandwiches, quartered into triangles. They were alone for only a few minutes before others arrived. One brought a vegetable tray with a cheese ball and another brought brownies. Mr. Barnes brought chips, pretzels and Ritz crackers.

The food was tasty, but George didn't eat much. He knew he wouldn't be bringing anything the next time either. If he told his parents about the food, they would have objected. His mom would have felt obligated to make something and his dad would have said, "This wasn't supposed to cost anything."

There were only two women besides Miss Noonan, George and Mr. Barnes, all of them at least ten years older than Miss Noonan. When Miss Noonan sat next to George, he noticed her feet and ankles wrapping around the chair legs again.

After they had eaten, one of the women said, "Martha, I read ahead some and that book is too vulgar for my taste. And it's probably too advanced for someone as young as George."

George was surprised to hear Miss Noonan's first name. He hadn't even thought about that. He recalled the initials on the note she had given him, *MN*. He assumed it meant Miss Noonan. Now he wasn't sure. He still had the note, though.

Miss Noonan held her ground. "I'm sorry you feel that way, Myrna. This is an adult reading group. I know George is young, but he has been reading adult literature for several years. He has even read *The Odyssey*. We are going to stay with this book."

"Well, I never!" Myrna stood up, as if to inflict her superior height over Miss Noonan, who stood as well. George jumped to his feet and Mr. Barnes stood too. George glanced over at him and saw a slight grin on his face. He winked at George.

"I'll help you get your things," Miss Noonan said. She went into the bedroom to get Myrna's coat from the bed. In another minute, Myrna gathered her pan and the remaining brownies and was gone. George never even heard her last name.

Mr. Barnes said, "Well, I'll miss the brownies. Let's get started, Martha. I can only stay a short while."

The other three discussed the first two chapters while George just listened. "Don't you have an opinion on any of this, George?" asked Mrs. Sherry, a woman in her sixties.

"Yes Ma'am. It's just that this is new to me and I'm just getting the feel for things."

She patted his arm. "I'm sure you will have more to say the next time."

Later on, Mr. Barnes began saying his goodbyes and Mrs. Sherry said, "Will you walk me to my car, Glenn?"

"Of course, Elizabeth."

They echoed their goodbyes on the way out.

It was then that George realized that he was alone with Miss Noonan. "I'll help you with the dishes," he said.

She gave him a radiant smile. "Thank you, George. That's sweet."

Then he noticed color in her cheeks. She was wearing makeup and a light lipstick and it hadn't been there earlier. He couldn't remember whether or not she had it on when the others arrived. He didn't say anything, just gathered up dishes and headed for the sink.

He was already washing dishes when she finished the rest of the cleanup, so she dried. After they finished in the kitchen she said, "It's only 7:30. Would you like to hear some music?"

He glanced over at a piano on one side of the room. "Sure, I like about anything."

"I didn't mean the piano, George, but if you'd like I can play a couple of songs for you. What would you like?"

George had been eyeing the piano while she talked. It was an upright but different from the ones he'd seen before. It was darker and shorter and had only two pedals, rather than three.

Before he could respond to her question, she went on, "It's a 1947 Starr piano, made in Richmond, Indiana. My grandmother bought it new not long before she died. I would like to have a more exotic piano, like a Steinway, but I am keeping this one until I die. It has a wonderful tone and it holds it tune."

She sat down on her three-legged, swivel stool, flipped up the fall-board, and immediately started playing. Her fingers flew over the keys and he recognized the tune as *Boogie Woogie Bugle Boy from Company B.* George was even more surprised when, after a few bars, she began singing it as well. He was mesmerized, and backed up without taking his eyes from her until he bumped into a chair, where he sat down. After seeing how well she could type, he wasn't so much surprised that she could play, as he was by her singing. She had a sweet, clear, strong voice not evident in her speaking voice.

Miss Noonan played a couple of fast boogie-woogie songs without vocals that George didn't recognize, and then switched to *Chattanooga Choo Choo.* Her voice rang out, *"Pardon me boy, is that the Chattanooga Choo Choo?__Track twenty nine___Boy you can give me a shine. I've got my fare and just a trifle to spare..."*

She sang a couple more verses and then stopped. "That's enough of that, Martha," she said as she folded the keylid back down over the keys. "Let's listen to some records, George."

He was still entranced, eyeing the piano, and didn't respond.

She said, "A piano is actually a stringed instrument, but it is also a percussion instrument. The keys manipulate hammers. Maybe you will learn to play one day."

George said, "I don't know about playing one but I will look up pianos in the library and learn about them."

Miss Noonan sorted records while letting the record player warm up. While she was doing that, George was getting other ideas. He noticed that she didn't seem so shapeless now. In addition, her hair seemed to have a luster he hadn't seen before. He still couldn't see much of her legs, but the ankles were slender and the bottoms of her calves were shapely. She had a butt, but not a large one.

They sat on her sofa, not touching, and listened to Guy Lombardo and Benny Goodman records. And they talked. She told him about growing up in Chesterton and visits to Chicago with her parents as a little girl. George was a good listener, so she continued, telling him about going to college in Valparaiso and then looking for a teaching job. "I had to teach in an Indian reservation in New Mexico for two years before I was able to get a job in my home state."

George said, "You don't look that old."

"I'm not old. I'm twenty-five, George." She pushed at his shoulder with the heel of her hand.

He said, "I didn't mean old-old. It's just that you don't look any older than me." They both laughed. Then he changed the subject and told her about Linden dying and finally getting closer to his mother.

She patted the top of his leg saying, "You poor young man." Then she blushed. "I'd better get you home."

They stood and George gripped her hand lightly for a moment. "Thank you so much for inviting me. I enjoyed this." He let go of her hand and she went to get their coats. Neither of them had anything to say as they rode to his house. He was glad it was dark. He would rather not have his parents see that there was only one other person in the car, a young woman.

At the next book club meeting, only Mrs. Sherry and another woman, in her forties, attended. Mr. Barnes didn't make it. This time, Miss Noonan had a previously prepared pot of chicken and dumplings simmering on the stove shortly after they arrived. Mrs. Sherry brought potato salad and the new woman, Claudette Fitz, brought a custard pie. George remembered how much food was left over from his first visit and ate his share. There was plenty this time too, and it was good.

Mrs. Fitz was the first to leave, saying her husband wanted her home early. Mrs. Sherry said she needed to leave too and asked Mrs. Fitz to walk with her to the cars.

George said, "I'll be happy to walk you both to your cars, and offered Mrs. Sherry his arm. Mrs. Fitz was in a hurry and reached her car, a two-tone blue Kaiser, first. She said, "Goodbye Elizabeth," and quickly drove away, honking twice as they stood aside.

When they reached Mrs. Sherry's car, a big, new, Chrysler New Yorker, she said, "You are a gentleman, George. Now you be nice to Martha. She is a good person."

"Yes Ma'am," he said, "You be careful driving home."

He went back inside and they were alone again. She'd already started washing the dishes, so George dried. While he finished, she retired to the back of the house for a few minutes. When she returned, she had changed to a shorter skirt and a V-neck sweater. He noticed the makeup too. While she was setting up the records, he was admiring her posterior. The skirt hem was still below the knee, but it rose up slightly giving him a better view of her legs.

Before sitting down, she closed the drapes. "This time we are listening to Lawrence Welk and Nat King Cole. Do you dance, George?"

George's face reddened as she sat down and turned toward him. "I'm sorry. I'm sure you haven't had much opportunity." She reached out and lightly stroked the side of his head one time.

When she put her hand down, he grasped it gently and said, "I would love to dance with you, Martha."

She squeezed his hand and rose, giving a small curtsy, while still holding it. "Martha would love to dance with you, too, George."

At first, he was awkward. He wasn't sure what to do with his feet and stepped on her toes twice. The song was a slow one and she pulled him closer. "Start by just swaying side-to-side with the music," she murmured.

It worked. He relaxed some and held her close. By the end of the song, he was in a cold sweat. "Could I get a glass of water?"

She smiled and went to the refrigerator, not seeming to notice his arousal. She poured him cold water from a glass orange juice bottle.

The next song was a faster one and the concentration of trying to learn the moves kept him in check. They tried two or three dances with slightly different steps, confusing George even more. Then they sat down to talk for a while.

"You haven't said anything about your parents since you've grown up," he said.

"Well, they're still living but they've moved to Chicago and I seldom see them. They've sort of disowned me."

"Really!"

"Yes, I'm an only child. When my grandmother left me this property, there's over twenty acres here, she also left me a substantial annuity."

"Wow! You don't act like you're rich."

"Oh, I'm not rich. I have to be careful how I manage the property and the annuity. That is just me. I am who I am.

"Anyway, my parents thought they should have gotten the house and land, especially my mom. My dad thought I should turn the annuity over to him to manage but I refused. It isn't that they wouldn't be able to manage it. Maybe they could do even better than I can, but it's mine."

When the next slow song started, she said, "I'd better take you home before we go any farther with this song."

George agreed, with mixed emotions. Neither spoke on the drive to his house.

When she turned in to his driveway, she kissed her fingertips and then reached over and pressed them against his cheek. "Good night, George."

"Good night, Martha!"

Her eyes widened.

He continued, "Don't worry. Tomorrow you will be Miss Noonan, again. You will only be Martha when we're alone—at your house."

She smiled.

George stepped from the car and she backed away. He didn't look back as he walked to the door... just in case one of his parents was watching. He need not have worried.

Two weeks later, the scheduled day of the book club meeting, the weather was rainy and the forecast was worse. George had to stand under the portico at the front of the school to keep from getting drenched while waiting for Miss Noonan to pick him up. She drove right up under it and he quickly jumped in.

She concentrated on her driving in the downpour and didn't talk. George kept silent as well. He was glad of the garage when they reached her house. As she exited the car, she said, "Please close the garage doors, George. Let's keep the storm outside."

The double-doors, hinged on the outside, were still propped open. George got wet stepping out to undo the props so he could swing the doors shut. When they got inside the house, she noticed his wet hair. She laughed and grabbed a towel. Rather than hand it to him, she stood in front of him, reached up, and began drying his hair.

They both laughed and he went into her bathroom to re-comb it. He hadn't been in there before and he liked the smell. A damp towel and a pair of lightly tinted nylons hung from a rope stretched at head-height across the length of the claw-foot bathtub.

When he came back out, he smelled fried chicken, but didn't see it. "I'm just warming it back up in the oven," she said as she pulled more dishes from the refrigerator.

"How many are coming?" he asked.

"None. The meeting was cancelled."

He gave her a questioning look.

"You were outside in the rain somewhere and I had no way of telling you. Mr. Barnes is out of town and the ladies don't like to get out in a storm. It's just you and me, Baby."

George didn't say anything. A multitude of thoughts raced through his mind. She bent over to get the chicken out of the oven and he had to turn away. As he sat down, he said, "I'm glad you didn't just take me home."

"Who would help me eat this chicken and potato salad if I had done that?"

They ate with little talk and halfway through the meal she took her glasses off. For the first time, he noticed that her eyes were a dark blue, a contrast to her creamy white skin. He had always looked away from the coke-bottle lenses before. Without them, she was pretty. See saw him look-ing at her and he glanced away.

After the meal, while he was washing the dishes, she excused herself to the back of the house. He was already sitting on the sofa when she reap-peared. This time she was wearing a shorter, light-blue, knee length skirt and a pink, sleeveless blouse with ruffles down the front. And, of course, the makeup.

George felt bad, wearing his overall pants, button-down plaid shirt and scuffed shoes.

"What's the matter George? Don't you like the way I look?"

"You look wonderful. It's the way I look."

She sat beside him on his left, took his left hand in hers, and stroked his hair with her right. "I like you just the way you are, George. But you do need some dance lessons."

She rose and went to the record cabinet. George tried to think of other things, squirrel hunting, pulling nails, working on his old car and fishing.

Before he knew it, she was pulling him to his feet and telling him it was a waltz. He kept his mind on the steps and started to synchronize with the music. The song ended and a slower one began playing. He pulled her close and she pulled him closer.

A bolt of lightning lit up the entire room with shimmering flashes. He saw their instantly repeated reflections on the picture window, like slow-moving frames of a film. The image of them embraced stayed in his mind, as if the lightning had burned their images into the glass. A cap-tured image, *like an old-time photography plate,* flashed through his mind. A thunderous '*BOOM!*' followed an instant later, shaking the whole house.

She squeezed him even tighter as he gazed down at her. She gazed back up and he kissed her, knowing she wanted the kiss. The song ended and another slow one started. They kissed again and hugged even tighter.

She pulled away before the song ended, closed the drapes, and then led him down the hall past the bathroom, past a frilly bedroom with a full-sized bed, to a smaller bedroom at the back of the house. This one had a daybed and they eased down onto it without speaking. They lay facing each other, her lips as soft and gentle as flower petals. He felt all over her body and she quivered with every touch.

He reached up under her already-raised skirt. She leaned back and began unbuttoning his shirt. They were both struggling frantically, and then she broke away. "Let's get in bed," she murmured." Then she rose, saying, "I'll be right back!"

George lay in the bed, naked, covered from the waist down. Only soft lighting spilled down the hallway from the living room lamps. Still, with the light behind her, it was enough to see her silhouette as she returned. She padded into the room, also naked, except for a small, black brassiere. He saw that she was quite shapely without the clothes. Her skin seemed to glow in the dim lighting.

She sat on the edge of the bed and he sat up beside her.

"You're not a virgin, are you George?"

"No," he answered.

She opened her fingers and a packaged condom lay in the palm of her hand. "Do you know how to use a condom?"

He started to say yes, but changed his mind. Instead, he said, "Not really," wondering what she would do.

"I'll help you. Just lean back."

He leaned back on his elbows and watched as she tore open the package and threw the wrapper on the floor. Then she began working the condom down over him. The sensation was so erotic he had to lay all the way back and squeeze the blanket with both fists to keep himself under control.

In less than a minute, she was on top of him. Then they were conjoined. The lovemaking was so intense his head was spinning. He tried to unfasten the brassiere, but she hissed, "No," and bit him on the shoulder just below the collarbone.

In another minute, it was over for both of them. She lay there quivering on top of him. "George, George, George. Thank you, George."

George was overwhelmed and couldn't speak. He thought about this being the first time in a bed, and her thanking him. The emotion was so intense he gritted his teeth to keep from shouting out.

She rolled off of him and said, "Oh my God." Then, "Stay right there. Don't do anything."

She rushed right back into the room with a towel squeezed between her legs, carrying a box of Kleenex and a small trash can. "Fold the condom into some Kleenexes and put it in the trash can. I can't have them showing up in my septic tank."

He understood and complied. Then he used the bathroom and cleaned himself up. Before long, they made love again, different, slower, and even better than the first time. He put the condom on himself.

Afterwards, he asked her about the brassiere. She said, "I'm small up there, so I don't like to show them. Please just humor me on this, George."

George murmured, "I love you," as he pulled down the cups one at a time and peeked. "They look fine to me. As long as I can feel I'll be happy." He reached his hand in and felt each one in turn. The small nipples responded to his touch. He had more in mind, but let it drop. She had already given him much more than he could have ever imagined. Martha didn't respond to either of his comments.

She still got him home by 9:15, but the drive was silent. The sky was clear by then.

His mother was still up, reading. She said, "I was worried about you being out in this weather, George." He kissed her on the forehead. "We waited for the rain to let up before heading out." She said nothing more about it.

CHAPTER 27

Fifty feet behind an outhouse, a killer sat on the ground in the semi-darkness. His back was nestled into the branches of a small scrub pine in the brush and weeds. He was a tall man and his upper body was in the open and facing the path leading to the outhouse. He was in the shadow of the moon though and the pine dissolved his human outline.

A large knife was in his right hand. This knife had been sharpened countless times, many by himself. It would shave fine hair without seeming to even touch it. He was waiting for one of the chosen.

The killer hoped it was the man from the fourth shack on the east side. This one owned a rifle, and he chuckled under his breath, knowing the man would have no thought of carrying his rifle to the outhouse. The man would put up a struggle though. It was expected and he looked forward to it, wanting him to fight back. The thought heightened the killer's senses. It was his second night of waiting, but he was in no hurry.

As he sat there waiting, the killer stroked the blade of the knife up and down the length of his thigh. The knife was straight-bladed with a hilt and leather handle. The blade he was stroking was over six inches long.

At one time, it had been seven or more inches. The killer didn't know the exact, original length. It was a KA-BAR, Marine fighting knife with a blade made and tempered from high-carbon steel.

Flies had fallen under the knife after landing on something solid. They always just fell over in two pieces. He got a big kick out of that. He imagined being able to do that to a man, chop him in half with a giant knife.

He was mildly surprised when his first choice appeared, and then quickly disappeared, at the front of the outhouse. He waited to make sure the man would be in there for a while before exposing himself. The man certainly wouldn't have bothered to go in and latch the door just to take a leak.

At last, it was time to move. The killer crept around through the scanty brush to the back of the outhouse on the hinged side of the door. He wanted his target fully clear of the outhouse before the man saw him. He wanted to be seen, but only long enough for comprehension. The killer wanted to see the man's fear.

Now the killer was in position, flattened to the front wall just beyond the doorframe. That side of the wall, not taken up by doorway, was just wide enough for his lanky frame. He heard the man straining and grunting inside and then the tearing of paper. *Sounds like a Sears*, he thought. His wait was nearly over. As he heard the latch release, he checked once more for the presence of others. There were no others.

The door opened with the man's fingers curled around the edge at chest height. When it wasn't quite straight-out from the frame, the killer reached out with his left hand and clamped down onto the edge of the door, gripping the man's fingers. He yanked it towards himself and used the leverage of the hinge angle and the man's grasp on the door, to spin himself face-to-face with his victim.

The other man was off balance as planned and had only a glimpse of the knife blade before it sunk into his gut just above the belt buckle. The victim still managed to smack his attacker with a hard left hand to the killer's good side, making the killer's ears ring as he ripped the blade upwards with his right elbow locked. They were about the same weight, but the killer was taller by several inches.

The man's body recoiled from the shock but even as he fell back into the outhouse, he made a feeble attempt to jab at his attacker's eyes with his fingers. It was too little and too late. The only sound the victim had made was an initial loud grunt from the violation of his body. Then the blade angled upwards and reached his heart.

The killer was elated. There would be others.

The following morning, blood-curdling screams awakened everyone in Papertown and the Rickson family. The screams came from Betty Hines, a short, plump, nearsighted woman who was a fairly new resident of Papertown. She had arrived at the outhouse just as the sun started to show itself and had almost stepped on the body of Clovis Barnett.

Clovis was lying in a pool of blackening blood, cut open from belt buckle to sternum. He lay on his side in a crouched position, feet on the inside just past the doorsill, the rest of him in front of the privy preventing the door from closing. Bulges of intestine were poking out like worms from a can. When more people arrived, they said there were scuffle marks all around the front of the outhouse. It looked like someone had caught him coming out of the outhouse door and plunged a knife into him.

Long before George's dad and some of the other men could restore order, the whole area had been trampled. Everyone agreed that Clovis must have elected to fight rather than call out. They also knew that he wouldn't have been taken easily.

Betty Hines was led off to another outhouse and her wails were replaced by sobs from Pansy Barnett. A group of women held Pansy back from the sight of her husband laying there gutted. Others had already taken her kids to the Schmidt house.

Someone said, "It must have been that sneaking Deeter Jompson."

It took all morning for the Sheriff to have the body taken away and to interview people. Shortly after arriving he called for dogs. The dogs milled around for quite a while before setting off with their handlers on a trek into the woods. Two heavily armed deputies went with the dogs' owners and all were soon out of hearing range. Now it was just after noon and the Sheriff was at the Rickson house talking to George and his dad.

"George, Billy Allen tells me you have a big knife. I want you to hand it over and tell me where you got it."

George's dad seemed surprised when George pulled the big folding knife from his pocket and handed it over. George had long before stabbed the point of the shank knife down into the common, Papertown chopping block and left it there. He wanted to see who would claim it. The knife was gone the next morning but he never saw it again.

The Sheriff flipped the blade open and inspected the hinge point and blade crevices closely. To George's surprise he sniffed the blade and then licked it with his tongue.

"Oil and pocket dust. I didn't think you'd done it, but I'll be keeping this anyway. Now talk."

George told him about the dog incident and pointed out that Billy still had a knife the last time he'd seen him. He told him about the shank knife too.

"I've already got Billy's and I'll be getting around to his little buddies too. It was a big knife that done this, bigger than the shank you're talking about," the Sheriff said.

Later that day, the Sheriff came back and said, "Well, Deeter Jompson is still in prison and has been locked in solitary confinement for a week. There's no way of him being within a hundred miles of here. Whatever trail the dogs were on, they lost it at the river and couldn't pick it back up on either bank, upstream or down.

"Ordinarily a husband or wife would be most likely, but we know Pansy didn't do it. Plus, two of the kids were in the shack with her all night. She remembers Clovis getting out of bed but drifted right back off to sleep. She said he would generally get up to unload his beer bladder at least once during the night.

"We don't know who done this."

This news prompted a gathering of all of Papertown and the Rickson and Schmidt families that evening. As near as everyone could recall, all of Papertown had been accounted for that morning.

"That don't mean nothing," Barney Allen pointed out. "Those dogs might have been cold-trailing a possum for all we know. The killer might be standing right here among us." He was right and everyone looked around uneasily at everyone else.

"Okay, Okay," Mr. Schmidt said. "We'll just have to be extra watchful and nobody walks anywhere alone, especially at night." No one else had any ideas so the crowd dispersed.

George's dad was very grim faced and hadn't offered his opinion. Later, when he and George were alone, he said, "This ain't over."

George noticed that the glow of a full moon cast their shadows as long and lean, but they didn't say anything more about it that night.

CHAPTER 28

George was in the woods for most of the day and had gone father east than he normally would have on his travels. His journey crossed the highway to the north side, exploring new territory. He had his rifle with him and had shot a couple of young rabbits on the south side, but wasn't really hunting. The rabbits lay where they fell, left for the varmints to eat. Now on property of unknown ownership, he didn't want to call attention to himself by firing the gun.

George had long ago fabricated a firing pin for the rifle by filing down an old square nail. It had taken several hours and a couple of nails to get it right, but now it worked fine. He suspected that his father knew the rifle was fixed, but wasn't going to make an issue of it. George knew that he was getting some respect from his dad, if not approval.

Since the murder of Clovis Barnett, George was openly taking the rifle into the woods again. Something else had changed since the murder. The Ricksons no longer used the outhouse at night. They used a metal pot with lid and bail that they kept behind a blanket draped across a corner. Before that, the pot had only been used when someone was sick or when the weather was really bad for a long time. Now it was George's job to empty it down the toilet hole every morning. After rinsing it with water from the back-porch pump, he would scrub it out with sand and rinse it again.

His dad said, "We have the cleanest pot around." This was one of his rare, private family jokes.

George zigzagged back and forth exploring the woods, occasionally going closer to the edge to keep his bearings. On one of the deeper cuts, he came across an old logging trail. It was very faint and led back toward the highway on the south side. He decided to follow the meandering trail to see where it came out.

The woods thinned and he saw that he was almost a mile past the Johnson residence where Carrie lived. George also noticed a gleam of metal through the trees ahead.

George was pretty sure it was a car, and not an abandoned one either. He moved in a manner that kept trees between him and the metal. As he got closer, he could see for sure that it was a car. A late model, dark blue, four-door Ford sedan was nestled among the trees.

Normally anyone might cross another's property or even hunt on it as long as it wasn't posted, but George still felt like a trespasser. Not knowing if anyone was in the car, George approached with caution.

Swinging wide of the trail, he skirted through the brush and trees on the driver's side of the car. If anyone was in the car, it would be the driver. If there was no one in it, they had to be in the woods near him.

There were both pine trees and fir trees screening the car from the sides where the lane curved in from the road. This not only kept it out of sight of the road, it gave George cover to make a closer inspection.

The car had an out-of-state license plate and George was sure he'd never seen it before. He heard a man's voice before seeing anyone. As soon as he heard it, he started to retreat, but then there was a second voice. This one was female and sounded familiar. He cautiously resumed his approach.

The sound he'd heard was a girl's laugh. It came again, and this time George was certain it was Carrie.

Inching within a few yards of the car, George was puzzled to see no one in the driver's seat. He crouched down and crawled on his hands and knees until he was behind a good-sized blue spruce tree that had branches all the way to the ground. This put him within a few feet of the car. When he rose part way up to peer through the branches, he was stunned at the sight.

The first thing he recognized was a black, *Red Ball Jet* tennis shoe. There was no one at all in the front seat, and the foot and shoe were poking up over the top of the backrest from the back seat of the car.

George shifted to his right for a better view. Carrie was in the back seat with two men George had never seen before. They both looked about twenty or older and had a city-hard look. She was on the back seat of the passenger side with her bare legs spread. Her feet rested on the seat-back in front of her.

One of the men, a redhead, was kneeling on the floor in front of her, and George could see his bare ass pumping. His head was thrown back, his eyes were closed and he had his hands around her bare hips. The redhead made panting noises like a dog on a hot day.

The other man, with dark oily hair, was leaning back on the driver's side of the seat facing the other way. George immediately thought of him as *Blackie*. The man was reaching across with his right hand in Carrie's brassiere, through her unbuttoned blouse. George saw that his pants were down too, and Carrie had his pecker in her hand, stroking him.

She was saying, "Oh baby, oh baby," with her head back and her eyes closed.

She'd said exactly the same thing when they had been together on the riverbank.

George was so stunned he snapped a branch off the tree and fell forward, his face only two feet from the open car window. He didn't remember even grabbing the branch.

Blackie, the man with dark hair, whipped his head around and stared right into George's face.

Carrie leaned forward to look past him just as the redhead between her legs said, "Uh" real loud, and then panted, "What the hell."

Carrie's face went from pink to red and then to white. The dark-haired man glowered directly at George and said, "SHIT! Get on out of here boy before we cornhole you." Then he threw his head back and laughed.

Regaining his balance, George noticed that Blackie and Carrie hadn't lost their grip on each other. He stepped back one step and raised the rifle, pointing it at Blackie's left eye as he dropped his face to the stock. The redhead was looking his way too now, but neither made another sound.

Carrie screamed, "No George, no!"

He shifted the rifle slightly, to an aiming point just between her eyes.

She clamped her jaw shut so fast George saw her bite her tongue. Tears sprang to her eyes and she said in a voice just above a whisper, "Please go away, George. Please, please just go——away."

George could see the tears flow freely from her eyes as he backed away. His last look was over the sights of the rifle. He kept it pointing toward the car until he was out of sight of it. From that point, he turned and ran without speaking. He held the rifle upright in front of him with both hands so he wouldn't be hit in the face by tree branches: branches that he couldn't see through the tears in his own eyes.

George had felt bad making love with Martha Noonan while still involved with Carrie. Now, his emotions regarding women and girls had him questioning the whole man-woman thing. He recalled how Eve had deceived Adam in the Holy Bible.

After four bouts of lovemaking with Martha, she had become worried that people at school were getting suspicious, and that her neighbors would wonder about her car coming and going in the middle of the night. "We will have to find another way to meet," she said.

"We will," He replied.

George had slipped out of the house at midnight for only one liaison since then. She had never said that she loved him and he suspected that it was just a physical need on her part. He knew that some women had a thing for younger men, or boys. Like Carrie, Martha didn't seem bothered by supplying condoms, and had a ready supply of them. Deep down, he knew that Carrie and Miss Noonan were worlds apart.

All of that had happened before his discovery of Carrie in the car with the two men. Now, George had not been with Martha in over a month. He still attended the meetings, but she always managed to find him a ride home with someone else. He didn't know when or if he would ever have another woman.

CHAPTER 29

George was sitting on his back-porch steps reading *Great Expectations*, the latest book club novel, when he heard a scream from the middle of Papertown. George was used to screams from over there, but not during the middle of the day. Thunder had been rolling in the distance and he tucked his book under the porch where it wouldn't get wet if it started to rain. He jumped up and trotted in the direction of the scream.

The screaming had stopped but George could hear excited voices. In the area between the shacks, he found Patricia Allen with her head on another woman's shoulder. Patricia wasn't as big as Esther Wales, but was still bigger than her chinless, snaggle-toothed husband who knocked her around some. And, she was bigger than most of the raw-boned Papertown women.

George was surprised to see that her knees were shaking. She was sobbing and clinging to the other woman as if she needed her strength. A few others grouped around them looking toward the Allen shack and kids were coming from all directions. Harold Schmidt reached the group just ahead of George.

They finally figured out through the babble what had happened to reduce Patricia Allen to a two-hundred-pound mass of jelly. There was a snake in her shack.

"The hell," Harold Schmidt said. "Just chase it out. There ain't going to be no poison snake in there."

"You're the landlord. You chase it out," one of the women retorted.

"The hell," Schmidt said again. "Come on George. You can help me catch it."

He started into the shack with George directly behind him. An instant later, George was knocked flat on his back from Harold moving backwards much faster than he had gone in. Harold tripped over the railroad tie step and fell down on his rump beside George.

"The hell! That's a big snake. I never knew they could get that damn big."

George had noticed before that Mr. Schmidt used the, "The hell" phrase a lot. He thought it was pretty funny when talking about a snake.

Harold noticed the expression on George's face and said "The hell. Come on then, boy. You'll see."

They got back up and started into the shack.

Harold ripped the wool Army blanket loose from the doorway on one side, letting light into the shack. He yelled! "There he went, under the bed. You yank the bed out away from the wall and I'll throw this coat over his head."

George noticed clothes hanging from nails driven into the open-wall studs all the way around the room. Personal items hung from other nails driven into the sides of the studs in the otherwise-unused space between them. George had seen makeshift shelves between open studs before, but not nails. Pinpoints of light shone through the tarpaper in several places where nails from the outside had missed the wood in the gaps between the slabwood of the outer walls.

Harold had grabbed a winter coat from a nail by the door. "Just be damned good and ready to get ahold of him. It's a big black snake and he's mad as hell!"

They charged toward the bed and George pulled it away from the wall as directed. He almost ran himself when he saw it. The snake reared up in front of them and its head rose higher than Harold's. Harold made a lunge for the snake with the blanket spread in his outstretched arms just as several people crowded into the doorway, blocking the light.

"Jesus H. Christ!" he bellowed. "He's got me!"

George jumped up onto the bed and saw that the snake did indeed have him. The snake's mouth wrapped most of the way around Harold's left forearm just below the elbow.

George was now above both Harold and the snake. He estimated that it was at least ten feet long and its body was bigger around than his lower leg. He grabbed it behind the head and got a good grip but couldn't reach all the way around with one hand.

Using both hands, he tried choking the snake. Holding it from the top with his right hand, he interlaced his fingers and squeezed its throat with the heel of his left hand as hard as he could.

The snake had other ideas. It curled around Harold's left arm and started a second wrap around his head and right arm.

Harold was a strong man though and pushed it up over his head with his right hand. It relinquished its bite on his left arm and Harold pulled free and grabbed its body with both hands.

"Can you hold him, George?" he bellowed.

George, who was dancing around on the bed trying to keep his balance, said "For a little while."

He jumped off the bed for better footing and saw that now the snake had wrapped its lower half around Harold's torso.

Harold said, "He's not hurting me there. Let's take him on out." Then he yelled at the bystanders, "The hell! Get outta the way! Someone get an axe or a corn knife!"

Doing a lurching scuffle-dance, Harold and George managed to drag the snake out to the cheers of bystanders. A couple of the women and Billy Allen jumped into the fray and unwound the snake from Harold's body. The five of them got it lined out and began carrying it to open ground. Harold had blood all over his arm from the puncture wounds but was still the strongest. He was able to relieve George at the head.

"The hell, boy. You might have just saved my life."

They both laughed, knowing that Harold would have gotten loose even if it meant biting the snake himself.

They dragged the snake out to the community chopping block used for chickens. It took all five of them to hold it while others went to get a corn knife and a hammer. It was too risky to swing at it with the double-bitted axe someone brought.

With George and Mr. Schmidt holding its head, they laid the blade of the corn knife on the back of the snake's neck and Billy drove it through with three strokes from a four-pound hammer. Even with all of them trying to hold it still, blood sprayed over several of the bystanders as the body continued to writhe from the death throes. Billy got it the worst.

After the snake stopped moving, they stretched it out. Counting the head, the snake measured eleven feet, three inches. Harold estimated it to weigh a hundred pounds.

Someone said, "Well, I guess it wasn't the Allens who was stealing my chickens after all."

They all had a good laugh about that, even the Allens. That night everyone who was willing to try it ate some black snake. They cut it up into cross sections and roasted it in the skin by hanging the pieces, backside down, over a bed of coals with pieces of wire. The only ones who knew how to skin, gut and roast a snake were the Ehlers' family. The Ehlers had recently arrived from Mississippi and were the only colored people in Papertown.

During the feast, people threw their skin pieces to the chickens, which amused them all with their running back and forth and snatching the pieces from each other. Everyone, including George, thought the snake was pretty good. It was a lot better than possum and tasted as good as, or better than, young groundhog.

CHAPTER 30

The tall, bearded killer lay face down in the weeds behind the chosen shack, knife gripped in his right hand. Discarded farm equipment parts and pieces surrounded him and his outline blended-in with the odd shapes. He wanted the man from this shack but knew he wouldn't be able to catch him at an outhouse like the last one.

The one the man used was too exposed, although it was some distance away from his shack. The killer decided to toss pebbles against the back of the shack to draw the man out. He was almost certain this man didn't have a rifle. The killer just hoped he would come alone and he reasoned that one man, even with a rifle but with no clear reason to shoot, could be taken.

Before he could throw his first pebble, he saw a display of light at the front of the shack, as whatever they used for a door was opened and then closed. A shape appeared at the side of the shack and he lowered his face to the ground as the figure slowly walked his way.

It was the kid. He wanted a kid all right, but not this one. He wanted the kid who lived in the house on the other side of the shacks, the smart ass. He wanted to make that one sweat before he took him though. Now, this kid was almost on top of him.

The kid was a pig-tailed girl and she stopped only a few feet in front of him. He kept his face down, only able to see her feet, listening for a sound of alarm. If she screamed, he would gut her like a fish. If she ran, he would catch her and silence her.

Maybe the man would come then, when his daughter did not return. If he did not come, killing the kid might hurt him even more. He could still kill the man later, while he was suffering the loss of his child.

The kid turned around and squatted in place with her back to him. The killer looked up just as she was lifting her dress. He couldn't resist.

Her bare butt was less than four feet from him and he knew what to do. In one move he raised to a half crouch and was upon her. Before she fully realized he was there, he thrust his left hand over her shoulder and grabbed her chin just as he had been taught.

She made it easier by starting to turn her head that way. He jerked her head up, clamping her mouth shut with a click of teeth. He arched his back and rose to one knee, lifting her off her feet. With a man, he would have used his arm as a lever over the shoulder. The child he could lift by the chin.

Still on one knee behind her, he passed the blade over her other shoulder, too quick for her reaching hands. The blade came under the crook of his left wrist, almost touching it. He drew it back and to the right wondering if it would sever her spindly spine.

The convulsion from the severed jugular and esophagus thrust her body forward and aided in making the cut even deeper. He felt the bone. Two whooshes of exhausted air from her trachea were the last sounds he heard her make. They fanned a spray of blood, adding to the huge arterial spurts.

As much as a man's, he thought. He felt a wet warmth on his knee and realized she had peed on his leg. He pushed her forward off his leg, swiped his finger across the pants leg, and then touched it to his tongue. He almost laughed aloud.

He wanted to wait for the man but as he pushed her body on over and away from him, someone opened the door of a shack on the opposite side, nearly catching him in its light as they stepped out. Ducking back, he wasn't able to tell if more than one person left the shack. The time for quiet work was diminished with the possibility of two people or more out and about.

The killer touched the back of his left hand to his tongue and then wiped the blood from his hand and sleeve on the back of her dress. Then he rolled her partway over so he could wipe down the knife on the front. With no muscle attachment, the head maintained its fixed position as the body moved from side-to-side. He withdrew through the weeds and junk knowing there would be others.

CHAPTER 31

The news of another grizzly bloodletting spread fast. The murderer had struck again. This time it was a twelve-year-old girl named Nellie Jenkins. Her dad Horace was the one who'd stayed with George while the men had dealt with Edgar Semms. The Horace and Haley Jenkins family was originally from Arkansas and was liked by everyone. Nellie was their only child.

She had gone out to pee around midnight. Her mother let her go with instructions to pee right behind the shack and to holler if she saw anyone. When she didn't come back within a few minutes, Haley went looking for her and found her twelve feet behind the shack. Her throat had been cut so deep that she was almost decapitated. Haley had felt the warm blood on her bare feet before she reached her daughter's body. Screams in the night woke everyone again.

Nellie was an auburn-haired, freckle-faced, fun-loving kid with pigtails and two big front teeth always showing in a grin.

The Sheriff said, "He must have grabbed her by the pigtails from behind and cut her before she could make a sound. He probably crawled up on her in them weeds while she was squatted down. It looks like she was facing the shack when he got her."

Someone suggested, "Maybe there's more than one killer, working together."

"No," said the Sheriff. "This is the work of a madman. No one else could do something like this and loonies don't work together. Now, damn it, how many times do I have to tell you people? If there's been a murder, or any other serious crime, stay out of the area. If the killer left any footprints or dropped something, you destroyed it. You come in here like a herd of buffalo and trample everything to dust. How am I supposed to catch a killer with interference like that?"

No one had an answer and most of them drifted back to their own shacks, mumbling under their breath. George and his parents didn't go to investigate the commotion. They knew they would hear the bad news soon enough. George noticed again that there was a full moon.

The Sheriff had sent the dogs and their handlers into the dark with instructions for everyone saying, "Stay home and do not interfere. There may be some kind of trail that can't be seen at night."

By noon the next day, everyone knew the dogs had again lost the scent at the river and hadn't been able to pick it back up. No clues had been found. Everyone was in a panic, convinced that this was an all-out attack on Papertown and not just an individual. Those who didn't have a piss-pot were going to get one or start using buckets. Some were even borrowing money to buy something. A few had guns and others were looking for guns. Some didn't want to go anywhere alone even in the daytime.

"That is too far-fetched," said others. "This killer only strikes people alone and at night."

"Yeah, well no one's sure what time Clovis got it and he wouldn't have been taken easy."

No one disagreed with that. One man asked Pansy to sell him Clovis's thirty-thirty.

"I can shoot it myself," she hissed into his face with clenched teeth. "I've got two kids here and I'll use it on you if I have to."

In the Rickson house that evening, George's dad said, "We're going to stick to our pot, and George, don't leave the house with it until people are out and about in the morning. We're going to do more than that, too. It's been thirty days between killings but that don't mean it can't happen again tonight. George and I will sit up in shifts tonight and tomorrow night, and then again for a few nights in about three weeks."

George got busy digging empty tin cans out of their fifty-five-gal-lon-drum burning-barrel that evening. He cleaned the cans, and his dad punched a hole through one side of each one, near the top, with a nail. They strung them together with string, several cans at a time. Some they set in rows on the windowsills and others they made into pyramid stacks to set in front of the doors when they went to bed. The loosely strung together cans would pull each other down if bumped, raising a clatter.

When George's mom had gone to bed, his dad said, "What about that rifle? You've got it working, haven't you?"

"Yes," George acknowledged.

"Well, I'll sit here in the kitchen with the rifle where I can see both you and the back door. We'll sleep in two-hour shifts in your bed. You stay right here while I'm sleeping. If you hear anything at all, wake me up. The rifle stays with me."

Nights passed without incident and George gave a lot of thought to the full moon during both killings and to what his dad said about thirty days since the last killing. He knew that a full moon occurred every twen-ty-nine or thirty days.

CHAPTER 32

George never saw Carrie again. He didn't know what happened, but when school started for the season, she wasn't there. He was still distraught over the whole thing and thought many times, *I'll never get over this*. Carrie had been the one he wanted to keep, the girl of his dreams. He didn't understand how she could be like that. He did not mention it to anyone else though, but somehow people found things out.

Pootie Barnett approached him again one day, while he was working on the farm equipment, and said, "Hi George. I don't want to see you get hurt but I thought you might want to know something. That Carrie girl you was seeing last year got herself in trouble and got sent away."

"What kind of trouble?"

"Not trouble with the law. They say her aunt found out that these old men were driving out from the city where she used to live. They were paying her to do it with them. Her aunt had her sent off to one of them reform school homes."

"Thanks Pootie," he said, "I owe you."

George hadn't thought about trouble with the law. He thought he was going to hear that Carrie was pregnant. He didn't know what he would have done then, or whether or not it might even be his baby.

The money thing shocked him, but it fit with what he had seen, except that those guys were not old. He didn't think he could ever trust a woman again.

Pootie shocked him even more a few days later. He caught twelve-year-old Pootie and fifteen-year-old Billy Allen screwing in the Allen shack. The grown women were all gone to work picking onions at the Holibert farm and as George was passing by, he heard a noise. Thinking some kind of animal had gotten into the shack again; he stuck his head in and hollered, "Who's in there?"

Billy jumped straight up off the bed, yanking up his pants and looking around wildly——*like a rat looking for a hole*, George thought. Then he saw Pootie trying to hide under the dirty blanket.

"Oh man, George," Billy was saying. "Give me a break man, don't tell. She wanted me to, I swear. I'll go to the penitentiary if you tell. Please, George."

George wanted to give him a break all right. He wanted to break his damned head. All he could see of Pootie were her, eyes, nose, and the top of her head.

George said, "I got one thing to ask you Pootie and you know I'll protect you. "Did he make you do it?"

Still holding the blanket up to her nose with both hands, she shook her head from side to side in a '*no*' answer.

"Don't tell, George," Billy said again.

"Shut up Asshole. I won't tell. At least so long as she's not pregnant, I won't. Not for you though, for her. If she is pregnant, you're going to pay in more ways than one. Now get on out of here so she can get dressed and leave. Go before I bust you up."

Billy left. George left too, just to follow him a ways and give him something to think about. A minute later he saw Pootie slip out and go the other way without a word.

Two weeks later both Pootie and Billy disappeared. A few days after that Pansy got word that they had gone to a cousin of Billy's in Kentucky, and gotten married. They didn't come back for a month. By that time, Pansy was so glad to see her daughter that she didn't even shoot Billy with Clovis's rifle. She told George later that she had thought about it.

When Pootie and Billy had turned up missing, George felt obligated to tell Pansy what he had seen. At first, she grabbed him by the collar with both hands and shook him.

"Why didn't you stop them? Why didn't you tell me?"

Then she released him and apologized for grabbing him.

"It was too late when I found them. They'd already been doing it and I owed Pootie a favor. Besides I told him I'd bust him up if she was pregnant or if I caught them again."

"What kind of favor?" she asked with a scowl.

"Not like that. She told me about some things, warned me."

Later, he offered to go with Pansy to Kentucky to help get them back.

"No, George. I'm not going after them and we're not going to be that kind of friends."

He felt embarrassed but knew she was right. She was a good person who hadn't deserved all of the troubles she'd had. She had been picking onions at the Holibert Farms to support herself, Pootie and Lenny, the remaining child at home. If Pootie came back with Billy and was pregnant, she might have two or three more mouths to feed. George thought that the Allens should pay if they did come back.

CHAPTER 33

The killer struck again exactly thirty-one days later. He walked in from the road and into the shack as if it were his home. Since he was taller than most of the men who lived there, he had to walk hunched over and appear half-drunk. A slouch and stumble seemed to fit a half-drunk man, although he never saw anybody moving around that late among the shacks anyway. He had been watching their habits for some time. They were so predictable it was pathetic.

Now, he would send them all in a different direction. This would be the best of all, at least until he got the kid. This time he was dealing with a couple. They were not the "chosen ones" but were part of the chosen place. The man of this couple was already out of the way. He was a notorious drunk and was lying along the road unconscious, appearing as a passed out drunk to anyone who might notice him. Most nights there was no one out on the roads this late anyway.

The woman was alone and things were quiet. Even the dogs were quiet. Usually they were barking but dogs never bothered him anyway.

They either sensed a fellow hunter or were afraid to call his attention to them.

He stood over her watching her sleep and listening for any sound of urgency or alarm. There was none. The shack was indirectly lit, ghost-like from a single sputtering candle stuck into the neck of a wine bottle. It was on the floor, tucked behind two stacked orange crates in a corner. He looked at her body in the flickering light and remembered when he used to have sex with women. He felt a mild sorrow for his loss. He would sub-stitute with this one.

The woman wore a long nightgown, raised at the bottom to mid-thigh. She lay on her back uncovered, with one knee bent and slightly raised. The opening at the bottom of the gown reminded him of a tun-nel, a tunnel that brought darker thoughts. He had been forced to crawl through a tunnel not much bigger than that for what seemed like an eter-nity. The thought angered him and he decided to destroy the tunnel as he had wished to before.

He saw her underpants lying on the floor and grabbed them up. Wadding them in his long fingers, he leaned over her from the side of the bed and grabbed her throat with one hand. He was already descending to straddle her body when she jerked awake. When she opened her mouth to scream, he crammed the underpants into it with the heel of his other hand and held them there.

"Oomph" was all he heard. He switched hands on the gag so that his right hand was free. She started thrashing under him, bucking and jerking. He drove a fist straight down into her solar plexus region, deflating her lungs. She stopped her thrashing and quivered under him. He let her see the knife as he pulled it from hiding. She was still trying to draw air into her deflated lungs and could only toss her head from side to side and roll her eyes wildly.

He casually reached behind his back with the knife and drove it down into her crotch. He had to twist it to get full penetration. Her legs hammered the bed behind him nearly throwing him off as she tried to push forward like a frog swimming on its back, her life draining away behind her. He rode her to the head of the bed where her head thumped against the wall and she stopped moving. Then he yanked the blade out, brought it to the front again, and slashed it crossways through the gown in front of his thighs.

He released his hold on the gag and lifted the top of the gown from the cut he had made and exposed her breasts. Holding them up one at a time with his left hand, he cut deeply under first one, and then the other. She still hadn't managed to spit the gag and he felt the energy drain from her even though she was still wheezing through her nostrils.

He crawled off and stepped back to survey his work and then decided to destroy the tunnel by slashing the gown from the inside, chest down. Not completely satisfied with the results, he inverted the blade and plunged it into her exposed chest, and then drew it down to the hair at her crotch. There was no longer any sign of life from her.

He put his hand on her bare thigh and felt the last of the death tremors. He could smell her steaming guts, urine and feces.

Next, he would do the kid. It would have to be good to top this one.

CHAPTER 34

This time the killer had gone into the shack of Billie May and Homer Watson around 11:00 PM and killed Billie May in her bed. Billie May was a short, large-busted, brown-haired woman with a round belly and skinny legs, making her look top-heavy.

The killer had apparently grabbed her throat and pinned her, stuffed her panties into her mouth, and then ripped her open from the crotch up to the sternum, going in under her nightgown for the thrust. The night-gown top was ripped open from the chest down and she was slashed under both breasts as if to drain them. Someone had seen the shadow of the man as he left and, knowing it wasn't Homer, raised the alarm. One of the deputies went into the doorless shack and found the body.

Again, the killer escaped through the weeds and brush, but with deputies hot on his trail. He managed to elude them before reaching the river, and by the time they got there in the dark, they didn't know whether he had gone up, down or across. Beginning two nights prior to that, the Sheriff had posted two deputies, one at each back corner of Papertown. This would have worked if the killer had come from the back or either side.

Instead, he had come in through the front. One of the deputies had shown himself in response to the alarm and speculation was that this let the killer sneak around him to make his escape.

Later, someone admitted seeing a man come staggering up the driveway past the Schmidt house and head for the Watson shack. The witness thought it was Homer coming home drunk again from Olsons' Tavern, which wasn't an unusual occurrence. Homer worked at Hastings Store & Station until well after closing and then usually stopped in at the tavern for a drink. Sometimes the drink led to several.

This witness's observation was not as keen as the one who had seen the killer leave the Watson shack. Everyone admitted that there were too many dark, shadowy areas around Papertown, even with a full moon.

On his way to answer the call, the Sheriff passed the tavern and found Homer Watson lying unconscious alongside the road. Homer was a short, skinny redheaded man with a meek manner and a grudging willingness to work. He was reliable, even though he drank, and always worked just hard enough to keep whatever job he had until he decided to leave on his own. Homer and Billie May were on their third stint at Papertown, having tried greener pastures more than once.

At first look, the Sheriff thought Homer was just passed-out drunk. While loading him into the back of the patrol car he found an egg-sized lump on Homer's head. His wallet was lying on the ground and some of his papers were scattered near it. If he had any money, it was gone. They would have to bring him around and then sober him up before they could even tell him his wife was dead.

The dogs trailed the killer again, but to no avail. As before, the trail ended at the river. Sheriff Parks was catching all kinds of hell, not just from Papertown but also from everyone in the area. There were more murders in less than a year than nearby counties had experienced in ten years.

Again, the Ricksons stayed in their house with their homemade warning system and silent vigil.

George's dad said, "Even if he doesn't come here to kill, he may come here in an attempt to escape."

They knew it had happened again just from the shouts, car horns and headlights coming from Papertown. There were even a couple of gunshots.

"The damned fools are going to kill each other," his dad said.

The commotion continued throughout the night and not a person in Papertown was able to sleep for the remainder of it. Every man, woman and boy over twelve was armed with something the next day, be it knife, gun or club. People struggled with emotions, threats and accusations from the stress of it.

Most of the residents thought someone in Papertown had to be involved or be the cause. The Sheriff had to leave a deputy during the day for several days just to break up fights. In other ways, people became closer. Neighbors who hadn't spoken for weeks or months now went to the out-houses together. Laundry was done as a community effort.

Those who had cars hauled several people at a time to buy groceries. Sometimes they would come back in the older cars with people standing on the running boards, the car itself loaded down with grocery orders from those who couldn't go. Hastings' Store had run out of baseball bats, bullets and shotgun shells.

George reckoned that half of the mattresses in Papertown had been slit open to get money for groceries, guns or ammunition. A sideshow of shooting contests sprang up, leading to betting and fistfights. People were tying stray dogs to their shacks for alarms, causing more noise, mess and confusion. It took nearly two weeks this time for things to die down and return to a semblance of normal. Some people had run out of bullets or money and others were just too tired to argue or fight.

Several of the dogs disappeared and George remembered rumors a long time ago of Papertown residents eating dogs. Now, he wasn't sure whether or not to believe it.

CHAPTER 35

With nothing else better to do, George cogitated about all of the murderous events during the long, night vigils. This time the moon had been on the wane during the killing so he knew it wasn't a full-moon thing. He thought about the railroad, and that maybe the man was coming and going by train. There were occasional hobos but the nearest railroad tracks were a half-a-mile away with no stopping point for another three quarters of a mile. Hobos seldom left the train and walked to Papertown where the residents were nearly as poor as they were.

George had also checked the train schedules his dad always had lying around. There was a train passing through on a thirty-day schedule that stopped a mile away for a short time, but it was gone within an hour. There wasn't enough time for the killer to make it to Papertown and back. There wasn't another train on the same kind of schedule to come back on either. He knew his dad would have already checked into this anyway.

For two weeks, they hadn't kept up their nightly watch and now it was getting close to another month since the killing of Billie May Watson.

"Time to be wary again, Son," his dad said. Pete hadn't talked to George this way, or in a paternal tone of voice, for quite a while.

That night they went into the now-familiar routine. George would doze in his day bed while his dad sat in the kitchen reading with the rifle either across his lap or on the table in front of him. They still had their cans strung up on all the windowsills and stacked in pyramids in front of both doors. His dad was confident that if the man came there, he wouldn't be so bold as to try coming through the front. The back was more secluded. The Sheriff had again posted deputies around Papertown, including the road in front.

"With everyone watching over there, it makes us more likely to be a target of this madman," his father said.

Two nights later, they got their answer.

CHAPTER 36

It was time to get the kid. The killer watched the house from across the road. He lay in several inches of water in a small ditch, surrounded by weeds. The water didn't bother him and there was no other cover anyway. He was very tolerant of discomfort and had conditioned himself to it. No one would imagine him being here. He had crawled across the barren field on his belly under an overcast, diminished-moonlight sky to get here.

He had waited too long and should have gone after the kid sooner. It was going to be difficult. There was a deputy posted seventy-five yards away, but he was sleeping, propped against a telephone pole and out of sight anyway. There would barely be enough time. The kid was wary now and never left the house at night. The killer would have to go inside to get him. He knew there was a rifle but he believed it was broken. At least that was what he had been told.

He didn't know why there was a light at the back of the house, or what the pyramid, silhouette shape on the window blind meant. People who left lights on were scared of the dark. The kid and the man didn't seem like that type. Maybe it was the mother. He felt charged thinking of this. He liked fear in women and relished the thought of the last one.

Now the moon was going down and it was time to move. This would be his boldest attack yet. The man and the boy together could be a rough situation but he would carry it out.

His plan was to attack, withdraw and then attack again. He would stab the boy and retreat just long enough for the man to reach the kid and try to render aid. He believed the distraction would let him sink his blade into the man and hang on. It would be a rough ride but the man would fall and then he could finish them all, the woman last. What a rush it would be for her to see them die and then fear for her own life. He could almost smell her fear.

He knew the kid slept in the front and this was where he would enter. He wasn't sure of the exact layout since the windows were all covered with well-fitting roller blinds, but he had watched their habits at night before taking the others. He knew that he would have to get in and out fast, but first he would have to deal with the deputy.

Even though the deputy was sleeping he was a large man, and not drunk. He had knocked out the husband of the last one by pounding his head with the hilt of the knife, driving his fist down like a hammer. One blow was all it had taken. He was sure that this wouldn't work on such a large man, especially one wearing a *Stetson* hat.

He would like to kill the deputy too, and he would if he had to, but knew the manhunt would be extensive and unrelenting for killing a lawman. He hadn't expected the deputy to be this close and hadn't prepared for it.

He felt around underwater for a rock. Not finding what he wanted, he worked sideways, back out of the ditch, feeling on the ground around him as he went. He had moved fifty yards and was about to give up on this direction.

He thought back over his trek and remembered crawling over a large rock in the field long before he had spotted the deputy. Time was running out so he angled back to intercept his incoming path. Once he had reached it, he couldn't remember at first which way the rock had been. He turned back away from the road, knowing that at most it would have to be before reaching the back of the five-acre field. In another fifty feet, he found it. It was the same size and shape as a softball, just what he needed.

With a much faster crawl than he had used before, he angled directly to where the deputy had been.

The man was gone.

He mentally cursed himself but resolved to continue. He listened for any sounds and just when he started to move again, he heard a noise, a muffled snoring. The deputy had moved for some unknown reason, but was back to sleep in his new location, closer to the house. This time he was against a tree and the killer could see a boat cushion under his butt. The tree made his hurried approach easier.

He made a three-legged crawl with the rock in one hand, intending to swing the rock around the tree trunk and into the side of the deputy's head just below the hat brim. He rose to his knees for a good strike and the deputy rolled around the tree to his right and looked up, straight into the killer's face. His hand was clawing at the gun and holster he was now laying on.

The killer brought the rock straight down onto the deputy's forehead just above his hatband, and three inches above his eyes. The sound was like someone striking a wet log with a sledgehammer. The hat rolled off the deputy's head and the killer could see the rock had sunk into the skull over an inch deep.

He was elated, regardless of the consequences.

Reaching around the deputy, he grabbed the hat and placed it on his own head. It was too big and he had to tuck his ears up into it so that it was snug enough that it wouldn't fall forward over his eyes. He felt the warm, wet spot at his hairline.

It was time to get the boy.

He stood with his head against the door for several minutes and heard nothing. The front had a roofless porch that gave him the room he needed. Moving back a step-and-a-half, he used a long leg to deliver a flat-footed kick to the door just above the doorknob. The door popped inward with a splintering of wood and a crash as expected, but only opened a few inches. It seemed to spring back part way. Something was holding it and he had to find out what it was. As he reached inside, he vaguely realized he had heard other sounds as well.

From 10:30 PM to 2:00 AM, Pete Rickson slept on the day bed with the rifle, while George sat at the table. George let his dad sleep longer than he was told too, but now he caught himself dozing and was barely able keep his eyes open. He knew he had to wake his father.

Except for a few grunts between them, they made a silent exchange. George went to sleep with the image of his dad sitting in the kitchen with the chair tilted back against the wall. Pete faced the back door with the rifle across his lap while reading a *True Detective* magazine in the dim light from a hanging bulb.

George had just gotten into a deep dreamless sleep.

He was jolted awake, disoriented, when the bed shifted under him. The motion was simultaneous with a loud crash near his head and a clatter of falling tin cans. For a moment, it was like trying to swim to the surface from a murky, bottomless pit.

His heart was hammering and he could hear his dad yelling as if from a distance. He dove over the foot of the bed onto the floor to escape the commotion at the front door. George glimpsed his dad leaning around the kitchen doorframe with the rifle extended and heard the shot at the same time.

There was a yell and more can rattling from the front door by the head of the bed. George peered over the bed he had just vacated to see a hand withdrawing from the slightly opened door. His dad was charging toward the door and yelling so loud that it even scared George, while attempting to load another long-rifle shell into the single-shot rifle.

Now his dad was fumbling at the door with one hand and cursing. In the background, George could hear his mother screaming through the closed door of their bedroom. George and his dad had laid a piece of two-by-four on the floor between the front door and the leg of George's day bed as a makeshift doorstop. This had kept the intruder from getting the door open more than a few inches, but now it was preventing George's dad from getting the door open far enough to pursue him.

With the frame and latches splintered away, Pete didn't expect resistance. He yanked on the doorknob so hard the two-by-four knocked the bed against George, where he was kneeling on the floor behind it, knocking him over backwards. The doorknob and shaft broke loose in Pete's hand,

The killer got away.

He hadn't gotten away completely unscathed though. There was a bullet hole in the door, near where George had seen the hand, and a blood smear on the inside of the door.

"I hit the son of a bitch in the arm," his dad exclaimed. "He was trying to reach around the door to find out what was holding it. I couldn't shoot at first because I didn't know which way you'd go."

His dad hugged him for the first time in many years, still holding the rifle in his left hand.

Within a couple minutes, deputies pounded on the door. George slid the 2 X 4 away and Pete pulled open the splintered, knobless door. Three deputies surrounded them, all wanting to know what happened.

Pete Rickson asked them, "Why in the hell did it take you so long to get here? Why didn't you get him before he got here?"

None answered and a couple looked down toward the floor. George could hear the hounds that the other deputies had already started.

In a few minutes, the Sheriff was there himself. After hearing that Pete Rickson had shot the killer, he was elated, saying, "By God, this time we've got him." He looked around at his deputies, whose eyes were now all downcast. His expression changed, "Where's Orloski and Johnson?"

Without looking up, one mumbled, "Orloski is dead. Johnson is with him. That fucker smashed his head in with a rock."

"You mean they're both dead," the Sheriff bristled.

"No, Johnson is staying with the body. Orloski was his best friend."

The Sheriff was wrong about catching the killer. Despite his injury, the man escaped again. There were muddy footprints on the porch and they led straight over into Papertown.

They looked at the footprints on the porch with flashlights and the Sheriff said, "Look at the size of them. It's a small man or a woman. Maybe even a boy. Damned if this don't beat all."

George's dad said, "It was no woman or boy. That was a man's hand and arm I saw, and he had long fingers. I shot that arm; remember! There's the blood."

It was 4:00 AM and it would be light in another hour. By then they had found out that the killer had somehow mixed with the milling crowd at Papertown, got past them, and was able to steal a car. There was no room to park cars between the shacks, so those who owned them parked along the road. No one ever locked them anyway and before they figured this out, several had left the area loaded with armed, would-be man hunters.

They found the missing car two days later, only two miles away. There were bloodstains on the door and the edge of the seat on the driver's side. The deputy's hat, with bloodstains and brain-smear under the crown, was lying on the floor in the back. For once, the killer had failed to reach his target. And——the killer was wounded.

CHAPTER 37

George waited until after the hullabaloo had died down the next day before beginning his own quest. Deputies were gone to pursue area searches of all the shacks in Papertown and houses in the surrounding areas. This left only one deputy behind. George's dad left for work and his mother retreated to her room after fixing breakfast. She was unable to cope with the stress and seemed to be on the verge of a nervous breakdown.

George took his rifle and a few long-rifle shells and easily slipped past the lone deputy without being seen. He reasoned that the deputies would have blindly followed the trail set by the hounds, which would again lead them to the river and a dead end. At that point, he didn't know about the stolen car. He was hoping to find bloodstains along the path pursued by the dogs.

When he saw that the dog's footprints led back into Papertown he abandoned his original idea and struck out through the woods toward the river. He reasoned that the man had to be going downstream or the water would have been muddied for the pursuers to find, unless he had a boat. George ruled this out as no motor had been heard and no signs of a boat launching had been seen during previous pursuits. Attempting to row or paddle upstream would have been fruitless.

When he reached the river, he followed its bank in a downstream direction, plowing through brush and skirting around raspberry and blackberry briars and other brambles, looking for any sign of the killer's passing, and hoping for bloodstains. He stopped frequently to scan the other side. There were places on his side where groups of men had reached the banks and milled around like lost sheep. The river was typically shallow with depths ranging from two to eight feet. The undergrowth became too thick so George waded into the river. He knew the deep places were just holes that he could get around if he wanted to wade across the river.

He continued his trek, wading close to the bank for more than two miles before coming to where low, swampy ground surrounded the river on both sides. For the first mile or so, he had seen rabbits, squirrels a few snakes, numerous turtles and an occasional deer along the levies on either side. The unsuspecting wildlife seemed oblivious to his presence along the river, as if he couldn't possibly exist there. He passed feeder streams and in one of them he saw a beaver working on a dam within fifty yards of him. It swam in a half-circle from side to side and back, looking at him as if to let him know that the trespasser was noticed, and that he was not significant, before resuming its arduous task.

He continued on, and as the levies diminished and the banks widened, the fauna presence vanished as well. Only the river at the center gurgled and flowed as if it was very much alive.

Slogging through the swamp would be virtually impossible. One would either sink in quicksand or into holes under the surface of the swamp water, or bog down in the mud. Only smaller animals such as muskrats or beavers ventured out from its murky perimeters.

He had no doubt that when reaching this area, both men and hounds would have stayed clear. George had never gone this far downstream before on his hunting trips either. All of the float trips with the Hartwells had started far upstream from this, so that they could float back towards their homes with the current.

Now he elected to continue and to take the route the others would surely have avoided. He knotted his .22 shells, his pocketknife and some papers into a blue, paisley bandanna from his hip pocket and then tied it to the end of his rifle barrel.

He had been carrying the rifle slung from his right shoulder, barrel up, with a piece of clothesline rope that he always carried for this purpose when hunting. Now, he moved the rifle up horizontally over both shoulders to keep it dry if he stepped in a hole. George then waded directly into the main stream of the river, clothes, shoes and all. He committed himself to going on, as there would be no wading out through the swamp and muck surrounding the river on both sides.

He went on and found the bottom solid. The current pushing against the back of his legs aided his progress. Staying in the center kept him in water from knee to hip deep, with an occasional misstep to waist deep, before skirting around unseen holes.

As the river continued, the width of the swamp around it expanded. At first it had been fifty to one hundred yards. Now it expanded to several hundred yards on each side in places. A sparse growth of stunted hardwoods dotted the swamp on either side, more than half with broken off trunks at a fraction of their once ordained regal height. The effect was eerily quiet. Water and lilies slowly swirled and danced back and forth around their trunks. Green and yellowish beads of seed and pod moved with the eddies. It was easy to imagine eyes of frog and snake camouflaged within their mix.

As George continued, all sounds of man dissipated. There was no more hissing of tires on pavement, fast crunching of displaced gravel. No chugging, putting, rumble or grumble, and no honking, squealing or screeching of machines or automobiles reached his ears. No voices, pounding, clicking or thumping broke the spell of nature's silence. Now the previously unnoticed sounds of forest and the gurgling, moving water were enhanced.

There was no turning back without an extremely difficult struggle against the current and he surmised that this would be so exhausting that one would be overcome and drown.

He was now more convinced than ever that this was how the killer was eluding his pursuit every time. After another hour, and another mile-and-a-half, George's legs were aching from the cold water flowing around them.

He rounded a bend in the river and knew that he was right. Ahead of him was a railroad trestle. Railroad construction workers had built it up on pilings high above the river to clear the surrounding swamp on either side.

It extended for a quarter-mile in either direction before reaching solid ground. The railroad bridge itself had no defined structure, other than cross beam, except for the middle section over the main channel of the river. This part of the bridge had arched, solid-steel sides that rose like a rounded crown on each side of the rails, spanning above the main channel. He guessed the height of the crowns at eight feet on the ends and twelve feet at the center. How they got them up there, and the entire construction of the bridge, were mysteries to him.

He stopped upstream in the middle of the river, tilted back slightly against the relentless current, contemplating the circumstances. He was four–and-a-half to five miles from home. If this was how the man was leaving the area, then he would have to be leaving by train or the dogs would have tracked him from one side or the other. George guessed that none of the trackers would have led their dogs out onto this trestle. They probably went around the swamp by road to resume their search for scent. He doubted they had come within a half-mile of this location though.

This meant to George that the man was probably still there. If the killer hadn't already seen him by the time he reached the pilings and started climbing, he would certainly hear him long before he could reach the top. The height from the water to the bridge was seventy-five to eighty feet.

George was determined to go on regardless. He knew the man had a knife and wouldn't hesitate to kill. George still had the rifle across his shoulders. His thigh muscles and his knees were hurting from the cold water and he wanted to get out. The only way was up, to whatever he would find. He checked to be sure the rifle was still loaded with the one .22 shell its chamber would hold, before going on.

CHAPTER 38

The killer lay on his back facing the sun. It felt good shining down on him after the long wade through the cold water. The world seemed to revolve lazily around him as if on an axis surrounding him and the sun itself. He marveled at how small and insignificant he was, how small everyone and everything he knew of was. He contemplated that the whole world might only be a flea on a bear's back,

The pain in his right arm had changed from sharp, fiery flashes to a constant dull ache. He had periodically waded in the river hunched over to keep the arm in the cold water and had left his coat sleeve down over the wound and had twisted it part way around to keep the bullet holes covered. He had been able to hold the sleeve this way with the same hand and didn't think the bones were broken. The bleeding had stopped until he started his climb and was forced to use both hands. He intermittently pointed that arm and fist straight up at the sun to help stop the bleeding. When he did this, everything seemed to revolve slowly around the arm as if it were an axis pole.

The killer heard a slight thud from below.

Sometimes a log would drift into a piling and he would feel the vibration. He didn't always hear the thud. Usually the sound of the rushing water masked any other sounds. The new sound was different and there were no vibrations. He eased over onto his stomach and crawled to where he could see down through the lattice to the water below. He lay there for several moments but saw and heard nothing. Not satisfied, he pulled himself across the tracks for a different perspective. Again, he saw nothing.

He knew it would be several hours before he could catch his ride away from here and believed the arm would be all right; and that someday he would come back to finish what he had started. While laying at this point his senses still told him something was different. He painstakingly crawled fifty feet farther from the center and found another place to look down through the lattice. He was stunned to see that the kid was climbing the trestle almost directly below him and was halfway up, with the damned rifle tied to his back.

The killer pulled back to where he couldn't be seen, raised to all fours, and gorilla-walked away from where the kid would surface. He would like to be there to cut his damned head off but knew that spot was where the kid would be the most wary. The kid couldn't know for sure that he was here anyway. Cover and ambush was his game and this was his territory. He would be able to finish the job today after all.

He crossed back over the tracks and slithered down between the ties like a snake. Underlying supports created pockets of varying sizes and layers and he knew where to lie in wait. To his dismay, when he moved to crawl over a support below, his clothes brushed against some accumulated stones on the beams, causing them to fall. *Spilled milk*, he thought. His haste had given him away. He knew the kid would undoubtedly see or hear the stones fall.

His failure to remain unheard forced him to move again and he had to crawl like a monkey, suspended from the beams above him, just clearing those below him to reach a safer point. This renewed the earlier pain in his arm and raised it to a greater intensity. He forced it from his mind and kept moving, but with more caution. Finally, he was satisfied that his ambush point was the best he would find.

CHAPTER 39

George reached the trestle and found the center support bases to be under the surface of the water. They were made from several creosoted, piling posts bound together with cables, the base wider than the tracks above. A central post rose from each bundle, tilted towards the rails as they rose. Timbers laced and bound together at the top in a crisscross pattern braced the pilings below the track underpinnings. The bracing spanned from the upstream to the downstream sides. This pattern extended down to just a few feet above the water. His guess was that putting the braces in line with the river allowed clearance for trees or other debris during flooding, or even the passage of taller boats.

He marveled again at how it could have been built and the rails laid. He did know from listening to his dad, that while laying track, a long bar called a *gandy*, its purpose to align the rails, was swung from joint to joint by hand. The workers swung it in unison while chanting or singing to keep the rhythm, christening the track laying crew as gandy dancers. A vision of men high above the river swaying and singing as they labored at the top, swinging a long bar, entered his mind. The span was high and long but there were no cross members from post to post perpendicular to the river until much higher up, starting at the mainstream edge on each side.

This meant that once he started climbing, he wouldn't be able to traverse toward either side of the river until he was near the top, but he could move in the upstream or downstream directions. He decided to pull himself up and out of the water and then rest. Once he was secure on the lowest bracing, he returned the shells, knife, papers and bandanna to his pockets. He replaced the chambered round with a fresh one, re-slung the rifle from his shoulder, and then started his climb.

While resting on the cross bracing, he determined that by hugging the intersections of bracing and poles, he could become almost completely hidden from either end of the trestle, but not both at the same time. It was noon and he noticed that the sun shining through the ties and headers created dappled patterns on the moving water below. The effect was almost hypnotic. Looking up, he could see only a maze of beams, bracing, headers and ties. Features were blurred from the sun shining down through them in rays. A plethora of hiding places existed up there in the shadows.

After a short rest, George began his climb in earnest. He could barely reach from one brace joint to the next and then had to pull himself up with just his hands until he could get a leg on the next brace. He was as quiet as possible while climbing, but still made some noise. At the halfway point, he heard something splash in the water below and glanced around to see what looked like stones falling from above and behind him. They had fallen from a point several yards away. He froze in place for several minutes. Not hearing or seeing anything more, he resumed his climb, but with more vigilance.

With the posts ever closer together, the braces were too, making the climb easier. A few feet higher, he encountered a spot of blood on a brace. The blood was still drying. This heightened his senses even more. He looked up often to check for any change in the patterns of light above him, or any movement or motion. As a hunter, he had long ago learned to distinguish between movement and motion.

Near the top, he stayed just a few feet below for a while, both looking and listening.

All was quiet.

He wanted to be sure that he didn't get his fingers slashed off when he reached to pull himself up onto the beams. Every level of support in the track-bed created more hiding places.

He worked his way over to one side so he could safely clear the ties and rails without sticking his head up through a hole. Upon reaching the level just below the ties, he found stones that had apparently been kicked up and then fallen from the passing rail cars. They were laying on the ties and braces. Now he knew where the ones he had seen falling came from. This gave him some indication of where the killer might be, if it was a man that had knocked them off. He scooped up a handful and put them in his pants pocket opposite the one with the .22 shells.

At this part of the structure, the bottom of the high, solid-metal sides rose above his head only a couple of feet away from the ends of the ties. George's senses were as acute as they had ever been. He looked at every opening around and above him for anything out-of-place. He remained vigilant as he quickly popped his head above the crossties and then back down. Seeing nothing, he pulled himself all the way up, then quickly un-slung the rifle before rising to his feet.

Once on top and standing upright, he had a different perspective. There were angled support braces leading up to the top of the steel sides that could be climbed, although it wouldn't be easy

Standing on the rail bed, the height gave him a slight sense of vertigo that he fought off by focusing on the situation. A man standing on top was totally exposed. If the killer had a gun, George would be easy prey. He felt confident that the killer did not have one, and he was hiding because

George did. George could sense his presence but couldn't tell where the feeling was coming from.

He moved toward the center, next to one of the rails, so the man couldn't suddenly pull himself up and over within reach. He walked slowly alongside the rail, looking at every opening he could see below him, and realized he could only see some spaces from the opposite side so he looked over there as well, knowing that there were places directly below he would have to look for on the return trip.

He reached the end of the metal sides over the river section. Here he could look out over the swampy tableau on that side of the river. It was a panorama of swamp weeds, lilies and brush growing up out of the water as far as he could see both upstream and down. In some of the open areas, he could plainly see large fish he guessed to be carp or gar moving around. He decided he would come back later by road, and catch a few.

Looking away from the river, George decided it would take a person running on top a long time to reach either end of the trestle from the center. He cautiously lay down and looked back under the bridge to see if the killer was descending. He couldn't see enough from that location so he crossed to the other side and did the same. He neither saw nor heard anything. Next, he went to the rail on the side opposite the one he had just traversed, and started a return trip. He returned to and passed his original entry point, growing ever more cautious. Still, he saw nothing and nothing happened.

Nearing the end of the bridge portion again, he saw a sudden movement in his peripheral vision and glimpsed a flash of light from below. He was already moving in a sideways jump toward the center when he felt a tug at his pants leg. While catching his balance, he felt a hot, stinging burn on his leg. He dismissed this from his mind, realizing that he had shouldered his rifle without conscious thought.

All was quiet again and George focused on the spot he had been in and the area under it. Nothing showed and nothing moved. He glanced down at his leg and saw a cut in his pants just above his boot top. He knew for sure that one wrong move could be his last. If he had been an instant slower, or fallen down, the knife would have been sunk to the hilt in his leg or body. The end of him would have come soon after.

Stepping back to the opposite side gave him more of a vantage point. He kept the rifle trained on the area of attack and slowly moved along the opposite side looking for a change in the patterns below him. Finally, he found it. At first, he wasn't sure what he was seeing. Through a six-inch square opening was a dark brown patch——a slight change in pattern and color. He assumed it was a coat, apparently over a person's mid-section. Nothing else was visible.

CHAPTER 40

Pointing his rifle directly at the coat, George said, "Mister, you're a dead man if you don't come out of there."

He received no answer and saw no movement. He set his sights on the center of the brown area and fired.

Following the crack of the rifle, he heard the tail end of a yell and then only some scuffling noises. He could see the man was trying to drag himself away under the ties. George noticed that up here the rifle didn't seem very loud at all, even though there was a ringing echo between the steel sides.

He reloaded and said, "I'll just put another one into you. You can't hide no more."

There was a wail from the man. Then he heard, "Jesus, boy. You done gut-shot me! You gotta get me to a doctor!"

"You're a lot closer to Hell than to a doctor. Now come on out of there before I shoot you again."

"Jesus, Mother of God, I'm coming, I'm coming. Don't shoot me no more!"

"If I do, you won't be my first!"

George kept his rifle trained on what he could see of the man as he dragged himself out to the edge, and pulled himself up between the ends of two long ties straddling a shorter one. The killer flopped over onto his back between the rails, his head toward George.

When George got his first look at the man's face, he saw a total stranger. He moved closer for a better look. The man was skinny, ugly and bedraggled looking. His brown hair, streaked with gray, was long, stringy and greasy. His face looked full on one side, but the other side looked as if someone had caved it in with a sledgehammer.

As the man grimaced with pain, George saw that the full side of his face had yellowed teeth with decayed gaps on both sides of them. The other half of his face didn't appear to have any teeth at all.

George thought to himself that whatever had caved that face in had also knocked out the teeth. The man had a thin beard about an inch long on the good side, and only patches of whisker and sunburned bare spots, spattered with white, on the caved-in side. The beard hairs were darker and didn't seem to match the hair on his head. To George he looked thirty to forty years old.

The man groaned and drew up his knees. He held an injured right arm up as if for George to inspect. He said, "I think you broke my arm too, you bastard."

George noticed the man was very tall but had little feet with ragged black tennis shoes a couple of sizes smaller than his own, and no socks. George began thinking of him as *Little-Foot* when he saw the small black tennis shoes with the white rubber circles on the ankles. Little-Foot was wearing an old, World War II, wool Army uniform jacket over a pair of ragged bib overalls.

He groaned again and said, "I've got two bullets in me boy and you've got to go fetch me a doctor. I'll die if you don't. I cain't even walk like this!"

"You'll die right here and now if you don't do what I tell you. Now who are you?"

"It don't matter who I am boy. It never did matter who I was. You've already judged me by who you think I am or what you think I've done, like everyone else in this god forsaken world has always done me."

"Where's the knife?"

"I dropped it under there somewhere when it snagged on your pants. Jesus, boy. I'm dying, cain't you see that?"

George thought that he was lying. He had seen two bullet holes in the sleeve on the man's right forearm and he knew for sure that at least one of the two bullets had passed clear through. Besides, the man had been able to climb to where they were. He didn't doubt the agony on the man's face, from the wound in his side at the beltline but this one wasn't bleeding much, which meant to George that it went deep.

George said, "If you don't do exactly what I say you won't live another five minutes. I'm going to give you a demonstration."

The killer had closed his eyes when he held up the arm, and he didn't open them now. He held his left arm outstretched to the side with fingers spread, while the right was still pointing skyward. George shot the tip of the little finger of the man's extended left hand.

Little-Foot screamed and shook his hand is if to put out a kitchen match. He was trying to shake off a hot bullet that wasn't there and what was left of the tip of his finger dangled by a quarter-inch strip of flesh at the last joint.

"Oh my God, you're really gonna kill me," he wailed. "You're a killer!"

George reloaded. "I could have already killed you. That was just my demonstration. Now get up on your hands and knees."

Little-Foot rolled onto his good side and glanced at his bloody fingertip with a shudder. He managed to get to his hands and knees but went into a spasm of dry heaves. George waited. When the killer raised his head, he was looking up the barrel of George's rifle. George motioned him toward the side of the bridge behind him and the man turned around. The mangled tip of his finger left a trail of blood wherever he put his hand down to crawl. When he got to the edge of the ties, he glanced back.

This was the first time George got a good look at his eyes in the sunlight. They were sunken and bloodshot but were also a startling pale blue.

"What?" he asked.

"Up the side."

"Jesus, you cain't make me jump!" Little-Foot squealed.

"Not off the bridge, into the train."

"What train?"

"The one that's coming by here at four o'clock."

George reached into his shirt pocket and pulled out a couple of train schedules.

"I studied them train schedules a lot while I was walking and wading, and finally figured it out. You've been coming in on a monthly but going out on a weekly, headed in the same direction. That's the only way. You've had to wait for the weekly two or three days every time, but this time it's the next day. I don't know where you came from, or where you've been getting on or off, but this is your last trip.

"From here, you've been jumping into a coal car, gondola or flatbed from up on top. That's what you're going to do again, except this time you ain't coming back. If you do, I'll kill you. If you don't do what I say, I'll kill you here and now___. Now, start climbing!"

CHAPTER 41

When Little-Foot got more than halfway up the angled beam with his slow progress, George scrambled up the next one, about ten feet away. He was surprised at how wide the flat top of the bridge crown was——16 to 18 inches across. He was sitting up there facing the center of the span with his rifle across his thighs before Little-Foot knew what was happening. George could see the look of resignation on his face as he struggled on up. When he reached the flat, George motioned him on up the incline to the top of the arch.

George said, "Lay down on your back with your feet toward me."

When Little-Foot did as he ordered, George scooted toward him without standing, until he was within a few feet of him. Little-Foot was laying eyes closed, with his knees raised and his left hand and fingers gripped across his chest with his right hand holding them. He didn't move when George started asking questions.

"You killed a lot of people. Why?"

He got no response.

"Did someone hire you? I know the people you killed couldn't all have done something to you. Little Nellie never hurt anybody in her whole life."

Still there was no response.

The thought of twelve-year-old Nellie Jenkins being nearly decapitated and the way Billie May was ripped apart flashed through his mind and he felt his eyes water. George waited a few seconds for his vision to clear then raised the rifle. He aimed right between Little-Foot's knees and shot him under the chin. He saw the killer's body stiffen and the eyes bulge, and then recede. This was before the tremors and the brief flopping of limbs that left him on his back with his arms and legs hanging down on both sides.

Little-Foot died without making a sound. George thought at first that he might flop completely off the top and down into the river. He didn't know what he would have done then. He didn't want the body found anywhere near this area.

He glanced at the position of the sun and knew he still had a couple of hours before the train would arrive. He looked both upstream and down, and along the tracks both ways. There wasn't a sign of life. He scrambled down to the rail-bed and then reloaded his rifle for no reason that he could think of.

George sat down and thought about things for a short while. The slash at his leg had put an angled thin red cut two inches long on the outside of it, just above his boot top. It wasn't deep and had stopped bleeding, but still stung. He got up and went to the place where Little-Foot had crawled up over the edge of the ties. It was easy to find, with the blood still tacky. He noticed a larger stain where Little-Foot had lain on his back. Apparently, the bullet into his side had passed clear through also.

He lowered himself beside the bloodstained area, to the beam below the ties. He could see faint scuff marks in the dusty creosote where the man had dragged himself underneath the ties. He searched for the knife for several minutes, but didn't find it. The place where Little-Foot tried to cripple him was within a few feet of where George had shot him in the side. The knife wasn't there.

He continued his search along the beams in both directions for anything at all. After half-an-hour, he finally spotted a small bit of white under an intersection of beams, two layers below the ties.

George had found Little-Foot's bindle. It was made from what looked like an old woman's dress or skirt. The material was navy blue with scattered small white flowers. One of the flowers had caught his eye. He cast around for anything else without seeing anything but the stick and a bag made from a heavy-denim pants leg. Inside that, he found a few cans of Campbell's vegetable soup and some navy beans, also a jar filled with what appeared to be water. There were no cooking utensils. George guessed that he might have cooked the beans in a hobo jungle and shared them with others. He opened the jar and put his fingertip in for a taste with the tip of his tongue, wondering if it might be moonshine. It was water.

Not finding anything else, he dragged the bag, the tied-up bindle, and the stick lying beside it up onto the surface. The bindle was as big as the medicine ball they had in the school gymnasium, but not nearly as heavy. He undid the knot and spread it open.

George was surprised at what he found inside the unwrapped bindle. There were two pairs of clean white socks, three pairs of boxer shorts, a pair of blue, pinstriped men's dress pants that George knew would have been far too short, and a polo shirt with horizontal, yellow and light-blue stripes. It was similar to one George owned.

A pair of brown, wing-tipped shoes that would probably have fit the man resided in a flour sack. They were the smallest men's dress shoes George had ever seen. In addition, there were fish-line and hooks, some strange coins and a man's ring and watch. Rummaging more, he found a few military medals, including one George recognized as a good conduct medal. There were some papers, too.

Some of the things really surprised George. One item was a letter of separation from the U.S. Army. Another was medical discharge papers from Mason General Psychiatric Hospital, Long Island, New York. Other letters were personal letters. The name on the military papers and on the letters was Vernon Naylor. The letters were addressed to V. Naylor, General Delivery, Monon, Indiana. George had never been to Monon but he knew it was a long way south of Papertown. He looked through the personal letters and found one with a postmark from Michigan City, where the state penitentiary was located. He opened this letter and was surprised to find:

Dear bruther. They have dun me rong and put me in hear wher I dont belong. All I ever dun was beet up 2 guys who was messin with my wuman. A man shood be able to kill anether for that. Wher we cum frum thay do. You no how bad it is hear an how hard it is on me cause yu dun time hear to. Hert them fore me. Get that cowerd Cloves Barnet that hit me with the rifle and that smart alec kid livin by there. Hert them all.

Yer ½ bruther

Deeter Jompson

Now, George understood the motivation. He didn't think Deeter, who was still in prison, had written the letter himself. He knew that Deeter could read and guessed that he would have been able to spell better but it didn't matter now. He put the letter back in the envelope and stuck it in his back pocket with one other. The rest of the bindle he bundled back up, knotted it to the stick, and set it to the side of the rail. The denim bag, he pitched over the side, into the river. It floated away, sinking gradually lower in the water until it disappeared.

He looked again for the knife but didn't find it. Then he slung his rifle over his shoulder and clambered back up onto the flat arched top.

The body of Little-Foot, now Vernon, hadn't moved. George had climbed up the brace beyond Vernon's head so he wouldn't have to crawl between his sprawled legs to reach the bib-overall pockets. He noticed the bullet hadn't gone clear through the head. The eyes were open but slightly glazed, the light gone from the blue in them. He folded the letter he had found in half, and put it in the front bib pocket, fastening the metal snap-button.

He removed the improvised sling from the rifle and pushed the barrel down into the top of Naylor's bib overalls far enough that it wouldn't fall out. Next, he scrambled back down to the rail bed and retrieved the bindle, securing it to his back with the rope, and then carried it to the top where he began a search of Vernon Naylor's pockets.

While checking the bib pockets, he felt something beneath them. A large *KA-BAR* knife was hanging down inside the front of the bib overalls in a homemade scabbard that looked like it had been made from two boot-tongues. The whole thing was hanging from a leather thong around Naylor's neck. The thong might have been made from the laces of the same pair of boots.

George recognized the knife as a fighting knife used mostly by Marines, but sometimes by other branches of service as well. They were designed for combat, but served as utility knives too, and were very durable. They were also plentiful and therefore, low cost. The blade on this one was over six inches long and razor sharp. He was sure that at one time the blade had been even longer.

He put the knife back in the scabbard and left both in place. There was no doubt in his mind that this knife that had killed three people in the last few months. He speculated that Naylor had probably killed others with it as well.

He continued his search and was surprised to find a second knife in the carpenter's-ruler pocket on the right leg. This one was a large *Case* folding knife, with two blades, each four inches long. One was a hunting-knife blade and the other was a boning or skinning blade, solid enough for beef boning.

The trademark double-X was under the name *Case*. He had been told, or had read, that the best of the older Case knives were identified this way and were rare, whereas the standard identification was with the double-X following the name. This knife had a four-digit number, followed by three letters, on the hunting blade opposite the name. The number was 5245SAB, and he resolved to keep the knife and find out what the numbers meant.

Both blades on this knife hinged from the same end and there was a factory-made hole through bolsters and frame on the other end. A cloth bootlace was looped through this and through the bottom buttonhole on the side of the overalls. He surmised that, if need be, the knife could cut its own tether in a hurry to free it for fast action. The bootlace was long enough for that. He had made a skinning knife in shop class at school and had read extensively about knives in the school library.

George could find nothing else of interest by going through the pockets. There was no wallet, no pictures, and only a few coins. He left them in the pocket he found them in.

George's plan was to wait until the train was below him, then stand so he could prop Vernon up and heave him over into a coal car or gondola car. He hoped to have time to follow up with the bindle in the same or a following car, but he didn't know how fast the train would be moving. He recognized that it must have taken a lot of nerve to jump into a moving train from up here. It was windier up here in the open than it was lower down.

When the train finally appeared, it was slowing down and a couple minutes later, he found out why. When the engine and several cars got out onto the trestle, the whole thing shook and trembled. As it drew nearer, the entire structure was swaying slightly, forcing him to grab the top to keep his balance. He was still sitting and knew that if they even saw him from the train, they wouldn't be able to see what he was doing. His body and dangling legs blocked any possible view of the prostrate corpse in front of him.

It was a freight train. Once the engine passed, there shouldn't be any occupants. If there were, the smoke and steam would block their view.

He realized that he would never be able to stand with the whole thing shaking and swaying, so he sat with his legs wrapped over the sides for grip, and dragged Vernon into a propped up sitting position, back against him. Vernon smelled of a variety of things, none of them pleasant.

George finally saw what he was looking for and gathered his strength for the maneuver. The quivering bridge raised his adrenaline and helped him with the heave. Still, he barely got the body to land in the nearly empty coal car. The gangly legs had almost stopped him and he had to reach around from behind the body and clasp his hands under the knees to get the right leg clear. It took all his strength to heave the body over into the slow-moving car and he nearly lost his balance.

It hit the side rail and hung there momentarily before going on down and out of sight. Moving quickly, George managed to reach behind himself and grab the bindle while watching this. He pitched it into the same car by using the stick as a sling lever.

Now the adrenaline rush was over and he had to lean over face down and hang onto the top with both hands. His hands were hanging onto opposite sides of the top and he laid his head on his crossed forearms, facing away from the train. Finally, the train was completely clear of the trestle and the shaking slowed, then stopped. It grew small in the distance before his own trembling stopped and he regained his nerve and strength enough to work his way back down to the rails. The trail of smoke and the scent of burning coal from the slow-moving engine still hung in the air.

He had found another letter in the bindle, referring to Vernon's time in the penitentiary. This one was from a woman. She wrote,

"Dear Vernon,

I have not forgotten you, but you must go the straight and narrow and get the killing behind you. It was purely an accident that put you behind bars for so long. I believe you when you say you only meant to scare the man, not stab him. You can be a good man again and visit your child some-times. If you will only find Jesus in your heart! He will always love you.

As always,
Myra"

George took this letter back to Papertown. Later, he dropped it in a place where it was sure to be found. He left the swamp by following the rails to the nearest highway and then roads back to his own area. He kept out of sight of the small amount of traffic.

By the time he reached home his pants and boots were dry but the pants and the bottom half of the shirt were stained brown from the river water.

For once, both of his parents were upset that he had come in well after dark. They were still convinced that they should all be vigilant in case the killer came back. George said that he had gotten lost.

He disguised the cut in his pants leg as a tear and explained it by saying that he had caught it on a barbed wire fence. His dad gave him a funny look but didn't question him. Well after his mother had gone to bed, and a long spell of silence, his dad said, "You don't expect me to believe that bullshit story, do you?"

George didn't answer and tried his best to keep a straight face.

By the next evening, someone had found the letter and turned it over to the Sheriff. Everyone in Papertown was enthusiastic that the killer was identified, wounded, thwarted and as good as caught. Tensions eased and the overnight vigils at the Rickson home ended for the rest of the month. Near the end of the thirty-day cycle though, George's dad resumed their watch and George didn't object.

By then, the Sheriff had inquired and found that Vernon Naylor was a drifter who only appeared in Monon, a railroad town, to pick up mail, which included a disability check from the government. The postmaster found only one letter in the mail that Naylor was overdue to pick up.

No one there really knew him and postal employees only saw him once or twice a month. It looked like another cold trail to the sheriff but Papertown residents were convinced otherwise. They believed that the killer had either bled to death or drowned after getting shot by George's dad.

The Rickson family continued their watch each month for another three months, after which everyone considered the killings over.

CHAPTER 42

Shortly after the killings ended, George's parents received word that his uncle Ward was still alive and would be returning home to the United States. A prisoner exchange had been made with North Korea and Ward was one of several previously unidentified POW's. The family anxiously awaited his return.

Before leaving for Korea, Ward had lived with George's alcoholic grandfather several miles away. The grandfather had recently passed away and, with Ward missing, George's dad had inherited the property.

It wasn't much. There was a quarter-acre of scrub brush with a four-room basement house and a shed made from the tan, metal van body of an old truck.

George's dad hadn't had anything to do with his father for several years. George knew that there were hard feelings between them, but didn't know what caused the trouble. They didn't live far away but George hadn't seen his grandfather since he was four or five and could barely remember him. Mostly, he remembered a gruff-voiced man with bushy iron-gray hair who didn't talk much. He had been a tile layer and had worked hard most of his life, installing tile to drain fields in the marshy, Northern Indiana ground. George's grandmother had died from complications of pneumonia when he was only a year old.

After the reading of the grandfather's will, George went with his grim-faced and silent father to see what was left of the place.

Earlier, George's dad had left word with the undertaker, saying, "Have the body cremated and stand well back when you do. He might explode from the alcohol fumes."

Afterwards, when they left the crematorium, the ashes were in a lard can on the floor behind the driver's seat of the car. They had picked them up to avoid paying storage fees. His dad asked the undertaker if he could have a refund on the price of the lard can if he returned it empty and clean. The undertaker, usually unflappable, had a perplexed look on his face. He never responded.

George didn't know if his dad was joking with the undertaker or not. Although stern, his dad wasn't usually bitter, but this didn't seem like much of a joke to George.

When they got to the property they sat in the car for a while looking around.

Finally, his dad said, "I just hope there's enough left to pay the property taxes and to recover what I had to pay the undertaker. Half of this belongs to Ward when he returns, so I'm bound to keep the property until we have his say. At one time, this property had value and there were valuable items he and Mother had inherited. I suppose he sold it all to buy drink. He drank before Mother died and even more so afterwards. There was a plan to build a bigger house on top of this basement at one time. He was good with both hammer and wrench, but he never followed through."

George's dad stopped talking abruptly and got out of the car.

The covered stairway that led down into the basement house stuck up in profile above the rest of the building like an outhouse with a lean-to.

The flat roof was about four concrete blocks above ground, with tar over the tarpaper, spilling over the sides and down the top two or three rows of blocks in rivulets.

George could smell a mixture of dank odors and see large holes in the roof as they approached. His dad yanked the flimsy top-stairway door open. The door at the bottom was missing. After a quick glance, he sent George to fetch the flashlight from the car. By the time George returned his dad had emerged from below with a shotgun in each hand.

He laid them on the ground and said, "I really thought these would be long gone."

One was a Winchester, *model ninety-seven, pump-model*, with a hammer. The other was a Fox double-barrel, with twin hammers and triggers. George had seen both in gun books at the school library and thought the Fox was probably the rarest and therefore the most valuable. He knew the ones with hammers were made before 1930, maybe long before.

His dad took the flashlight and went below again, saying, "Keep an eye on things up here, and don't go down there. It's not safe."

George listened to him crashing around below for a few minutes, and then went over to the old truck-bed shed. It was an enclosed metal body with double doors, sitting flat on the ground. George found that it was unlocked and rotated the locking handle mechanism that opened the right-side door. The latches at top and bottom grated, breaking their bonds of rust. Opening this door released the other door too. This door hadn't been opened in years and he had to pull hard. It came open with a screech like a nail pulled from oak lumber. George found the shed filled with spiders and junk of all kinds piled to the ceiling.

Checking to be sure there was no one else around, he began moving out the easiest to carry, larger items. There were floor lamps, wooden chairs, boxes of glasses, dishes and a wooden wheelbarrow with a broken wooden wheel. Every inch of space seemed to hold something. Items were stacked under, around and in-between each other. Several damp, cardboard boxes on the floor held clothes.

Next, he carried out odd tools, leather aprons, harness, and a saddle. Long, thin, tapered boards of varying sizes were propped against one wall. He knew these were used for stretching the pelts of trapped muskrat, fox, coon or possum. There were small ones too, ranging in size from weasel to mink or rabbit. Old Man James had shown him similar boards and explained their use.

George found nothing else to interest him until he reached a corner. Under a leaning stack of wooden garden stakes, he saw a three-gallon bucket with rags in it. Moving the stakes to get at the bucket, he found something else. Mixed in with the stakes was a rifle covered in burlap. Removing this first, he found an oilcloth under the burlap, and then a layer of oiled rags.

The rifle he uncovered was in excellent condition. George had never seen one before, but he knew that it was a bolt-action target rifle. He had studied guns and military weapons in the school library too. Closer inspection showed it to be a *Mossberg Model 35A, Caliber 22LR*. He raised it to see what a heavy barreled rifle would feel like. The weight and balance felt natural and secure to him.

"That'll be mine or Wards. Now keep an eye on things like I told you too," the voice behind him said.

He handed the rifle to his dad, startled and embarrassed that he had been caught by surprise. His dad took the rifle and laid it beside the two shotguns he had found, and then went back into the basement house. George rewrapped the rifle as he had found it. He noticed that other items had been laid out while he had been in the shed. He remembered the bucket in the corner and went back to retrieve it.

When he lifted the bucket, he could tell it was more than rags. Beneath them, he found another oilcloth wrapped package. Inside this oilcloth was an oil-soaked rag wrapped around a revolver. It was in good condition and had black, hard rubber grips. It was marked *U.S. Revolver Co. Cal 38* on the barrel. George was keeping a closer eye this time and knew from sounds that his dad was still in the basement house. He re-wrapped the revolver and placed it outside with the long guns.

Returning to the shed, he found cigar boxes full of letters and red *Prince Albert* cans with foreign currency in them. These items he laid out with the others his dad had removed from the house. He noticed one of the items was a locked metal box about a foot square and six inches high.

His dad loaded the locked box, all four guns, and the tins with letters and currency into the trunk of the car. He had George move the rest of the items back into the shed.

After that day, George never saw any of the items Pete took home again. His dad never retrieved any furniture or clothing. When he came up from his last trip he said, "I'd like to burn the damned place but its half Wards, so we won't. It's a wonder it wasn't all stolen." He produced a padlock and locked the shed.

The rest of the day they spent patching the holes in the roof with pieces of tin and buckets of tar they had found, apparently left there for that purpose. They had difficulty opening the buckets of old tar, but once opened, the tar inside was workable.

CHAPTER 43

Ward Rickson returned from his second tour of duty in Korea a very different man from when he left. At twenty-one years old, he now looked forty. He was skinny with a gaunt face, receding hairline and had a haunted look. The North Koreans had tattooed dots on his arm identifying him forever as their captive. He seemed to have no interest in spending time alone with George, who didn't try to force himself on his uncle.

When Ward was told of the father's death and the property recovered, he said, "There's no way I'm going to ever live underground again. I'll empty the shed and live in that if I have to and until I can build something else."

They helped him empty it, taking some things with them. George and his dad carried other stuff down into the basement house, where Ward wouldn't go. George knew that the North Koreans had kept Ward in a hole in the frozen ground. He heard his parents talking about him having to stay crouched below the frost line to survive.

Ward lived in the shed for quite a while with one or both doors open night and day, rain or shine.

He agreed to divide the personal property with George's dad and bought his share of the real estate from him with some of his military settlement.

Once they had removed all they could find of value from the basement house, Ward wanted to do the rest alone. Later they found that he had torn down the above ground entrance, caved in the roof and broke off the top rows of blocks with a sledgehammer. He filled the whole thing in with sand from nearby using only a shovel and a steel-wheeled wheelbarrow he'd gotten somewhere.

George would walk over occasionally, but Ward pretty much ignored him, so he left. Later, he saw that Ward had built a wooden shack, with a high peaked roof and windows on all sides, at the back edge of the property. It was bigger than the shacks in Papertown and Ward had covered the outside with green, overlapping, roll siding applied horizontally.

Once when George stopped by, it started to rain and Ward let him into the shack. The inside walls were made from thin plywood, buckled in some places, painted chalk-white. The interior was one big room with a bed, chest of drawers and a rocking chair on one side. The other side supported a porcelain sink mounted on a wooden-framed platform. A hand pump was mounted on a pipe coming up through the floor and platform. George didn't know how he had drilled the well and didn't ask. The platform had shelving underneath and the whole thing was skirted with a red and white checkered oilcloth hanging almost to the floor. The skirting looked out of place compared to its surroundings. A small, shellacked wooden table sat in the center, accompanied by two mismatched wooden chairs.

The floor was bare, rough-lumber boards with throw rugs beside the bed and at the doors. There were doors at both front and back of the shack, but near the back door a railroad-caboose, potbelly *wood-or-coal stove* blocked the way. You had to walk around it to get to the door. Firewood boxes with stove wood were on either side of the door, making it more crowded. Ward used the stove for both heat and cooking.

Ward offered George bread with lard on it but he wouldn't eat it, so Ward ate it himself and then opened a can of peaches with a little folding military can-opener he called a *John Wayne P-thirty-eight*. They shared the peaches silently. George ate his from a cup with a spoon and Ward ate his from the can with a fork, and then drank the remaining juice straight from the can.

There was no real conversation. George told him about the fight with Junior Semms and the beating he had taken from Deeter Jompson.

Ward only grunted a couple of times during the tales, and didn't speak until George finished. Then he said, "The only good fight is the one you ain't in." He stepped over and swung the door all the way open, motioning George to leave. He remained reclusive from then on. His old Chevy sat under a pine tree on the property where it had been while he was gone. George never did see his uncle drive it again, although he knew that he must have.

CHAPTER 44

It was six months before word of the body of Vernon Naylor reached Papertown. He had been buried under a hundred tons of coal through an unknown number of refills and the body was pretty well torn up when it was found. The coal dust had slowed the normal decaying process. Part of the time lapse was in connecting the corpse to Papertown. No mention was made of bullet wounds. Identification was based primarily on a tattered letter found in the top pocket of the bib overalls.

Sheriff Parks drove out to Papertown on a Saturday morning, and standing on the Rickson property line, made a short declaration. "This Vernon Naylor was Deeter Jompson's half-brother. Head injuries during the war caused him to be mentally incapacitated. Despite that, psychiatrists deemed him fit to release back into society, even though he had a criminal record before the injury and before the draft board took him.

"Deeter Jompson took advantage of that to seek vengeance on all of you, and there is proof of that. Jompson is still in prison and he will serve more time for that. He'll be an old, old man before he gets out—if ever."

That spring George celebrated his 18th birthday and a few weeks after that, graduated from high school. Following the ceremony, he told his dad that as soon as he got the car running, he would go find a full-time job.

His dad motioned him out onto the porch where they could talk alone and said, "I already told your mother you'd be going off to the Army when you finished school and you just hated to tell her. Say your good-byes to her and whoever else Sunday. I'll take you to the depot Monday morning. It's all set."

George was surprised, but didn't object or ask why. Pete went back inside, leaving George on the porch to contemplate matters. He did have goodbyes for some of the people in Papertown and for the Schmidts, so he went on over there. Mrs. Schmidt gave him a whole apple pie to take on his trip.

As promised, his dad drove him to town early Monday morning. George's mother was the last and hardest to leave behind. Rather than going to the depot though, they went to Sheriff Parks' house. The Sheriff was waiting for them and climbed into the back seat.

"Hello George," was all he said.

They continued on, with George's dad and Sheriff Parks talking of everything but where they were going, while George, riding in front, said nothing. After what seemed like hours to George, they reached Indianapolis, where his dad drove to an Armed Forces Recruiting Center.

The Sheriff waited in the car while George's dad escorted him to the door. There, he shook George's hand and gave him ten dollars, then wished him good luck. "Don't forget to write to your mother," he said as he walked back to the car.

CHAPTER 45

Eleven months later George was in Vietnam, a place he had never heard of before leaving home. Now he was a Private First Class climbing a remote, jungle-like hillside and carrying sixty pounds of gear. A bony sergeant named Stample, with big ears and a wide mouth, was right behind him, carrying even more gear. Stample wasn't George's platoon sergeant. He had been taken to meet Stample on an overcast afternoon.

Prior to this, and shortly after arriving in Vietnam, George and two others had been singled out, driven to a small, strange military camp in the jungle, and pointed toward a twenty-man tent where they had been told by an NCO to, "Stay low, keep your head down, and your mouth shut."

Most of the American soldiers around them were unshaven and dressed in a variety of mismatched uniforms. They didn't talk to George or the other two. After four days of sitting around repeatedly cleaning weapons, a corporal woke George from a nap and drove him in a Jeep to a different camp several miles from the compound. There, he met Sergeant Stample in a similar tent.

When George met him, there were several other men present, but he wasn't introduced to them. Two of them were in dark civilian clothes with non-military boots. George had the impression that one of them was French, although the man never spoke in his presence.

Shortly after arriving in Vietnam, George had received a letter from his mother telling him that one of the Papertown trash had set fire to some of the shacks and three had burned down. Billy Allen had become a hero, dragging a woman and two children out of a burning shack to safety. The children had tried to hide from the fire by dragging the mattress from the floor, up over them. They were huddled in a corner and the mother had gone back into the fire looking for them. She had already taken the baby outside and handed it to someone before going back for the other two. When she didn't come out, Billy went in after her and found the two children by working his way around the walls on his hands and knees. On the way out he tripped over the mother, who was crawling around in a daze in the smoke.

When he went back for her, she fought him, causing both of them to get badly burned when part of the roof caved in, and melted tarpaper, fell on them. She hadn't realized the children were already out.

The Sawmill had closed and most of the shacks were empty from people leaving to go farther north for work.

"*Good riddance to them*," his mother said in her letter.

George received another letter just a few days later. This one was from Harold Schmidt. A part of the letter was to let George know that Mrs. Schmidt had passed away. She had totally lost her appetite and finally could eat nothing.

Their doctor diagnosed her as having appendicitis, but when they opened her up to remove the appendix, they found a tumor as big as a muskmelon in her abdomen. They attempted to remove the tumor, but she died during the surgery. The doctor listed the cause of death as cancer and septic shock. This had happened three months previously.

Harold went on to say how he missed having George around and praised him for helping to keep things on an even keel in Papertown while he was there. The letter ended on a positive note saying that Pansy Barnett and her youngest child, Lenny, had moved into the upstairs apartment. She was his new housekeeper.

Billy and Pootie Allen stayed in the shack she had been in and Billy had George's old job as farm mechanic, although George could have it back if he got out of the service and wanted it. He ended the letter by saying that he and Pansy would soon be married.

Stample's voice brought him back to the present. The corporal had taken George into the tent and left him alone there, where he sat on a folding chair waiting to see what was going to happen. Minutes later, several men entered, only one wearing insignia. Stample stepped forward saying, "I'm Stample, your new sergeant. Listen to what these men tell you." George had jumped to his feet and stood at attention, but didn't salute.

Only one spoke, the taller of two who were wearing civilian clothes. George suspected he was a high-ranking officer but said nothing.

The man looked straight into his eyes and said, "It's a white man we're after. Does that bother you?"

"No," George said. Then, looking straight back at the man he completed his thoughts and said, "No sir it doesn't."

"Good He's a rogue, a deserter and a traitor. Any questions?"

"No sir."

The man grunted then glanced at the French-looking man who merely shrugged.

They both left. Afterwards, Stample and another man in uniform, but without a name tag or insignia, showed him black and white and color pictures of a different man. He was surprised to see the man in the pictures was wearing a U.S. Army uniform. In some photos, he was wearing khakis and in others fatigues. He had reddish hair and staff sergeant's stripes.

George could make out the name Harmon on the white cloth nametag on the fatigues. He had noticed the name Harmon, John Jackson on papers in the folder when they removed the pictures. The unnamed soldier hurriedly covered the papers when he saw George glance at them.

In some of the black and white pictures, Harmon was in civilian clothing in a fire-lit jungle setting at night. He was with several Asian men in uniforms. Four white men were in a row, tied and kneeling with heads hanging. One was wearing a uniform that was foreign to George. He had dark hair and a goatee. On the other three, George could identify U.S. Army boots and fatigue pants.

The prisoners were shirtless and on the clean-shaven men, he could see their taped-up dog tags. Each man had one hanging from a thong around his neck and the other woven into a bootlace. One of the photographs showed Harmon with a fistfull of a tied GI's hair while kicking the man in the groin. George had seen enough.

The men around George seemed to sense this and the taller one said, "That's it."

CHAPTER 46

Stample said, "I heard you have one of the highest range scores the Army ever had in basic, and the profile to go along with it."

George stopped in his tracks, causing Stample to almost crash into him. "What do you mean by that?" he asked.

"Nothing kid. I just want to make sure you can do the job. My ass is hanging out here, too."

"I'll do the job. Don't call me kid——Sergeant."

Stample didn't say any more for a while. Then finally he said, "We ain't even in a war in this country, at least not yet. The Frogs are still moving out and then it'll be our turn to get our asses handed to us."

George didn't answer and Stample didn't seem to expect him to.

They had been ferried into the jungle in a UH-1B helicopter that made a very brief night landing, pinpointed by pink and blue smoke grenades. As soon as their gear was dumped out, the helicopter left. George and Stample packed it all on each other's backs and had hiked, hacked and climbed for two-and-a-half hours in the dark before reaching the top of the hill designated on their map. They eased up to the crest for a look as dawn was breaking. Below them was a military camp that could only be North Vietnamese Army.

Stample whispered, though they were more than seven hundred and fifty yards away. "Our intel says he'll be getting into a truck in about twenty minutes."

George built up his rest and they settled down to wait. Stample had the spotting scope and George had his M-1 sniper rifle. As big as it was, the M-1 was still his favorite, even with the offset scope mounting and top ejection. It also had a tendency to smash your thumb when you closed the bolt without a round in the chamber if you weren't careful. George had gotten an *M1-Thumb* only once, during basic training.

Now, people were moving below them and the target had appeared. George settled in and Stample put a hand on his shoulder.

He whispered, "You can call it off and nothing will happen to you——I just want you to be sure. That's a human being down there and this shot will change your life forever."

Less than a minute later, George squeezed off his shot.

George Rickson had found a new home.

Many thanks to all of those who have read my stories, supported and encouraged me, and most of all to those who really dug into my work.

Daddy' Dave Grimmett __ Author, Professor, PE

Anna __ World Traveler, Professor, Author

Frank Allan Rogers __ Author, Traveler, Entrepreneur

Jerry Smith __ US Army Ret. RIP

BadBob Johnson __ USMC Ret. RIP

Nashville Writers Meetup

Clarksville Writers Meetup

Janie Broadhead __ Beta Reader, Sweetheart, Friend

Sara Smith __ Beta Reader, Friend

Any and all mistakes are mine alone. I refuse to share them!

ABOUT THE AUTHOR

Dave Norem is a retired manufacturing engineer and jack-of-all-trades. He lives in Clarksville, Tennessee.

Dave has ridden alone over most of the Continental U S on a motorcycle, walked alone in strange cities at night - in ethnic areas of large cities – in forests at night – and in foreign lands. His short stories have been published in magazines and anthologies. His previous novel, RECURRENCE, received the *Readers' Favorite* Five Star Award in all five categories.